Hala kh Najim

A Contrastive Functional Grammar of English and Arabic

Hala kh Najim

A Contrastive Functional Grammar of English and Arabic

From Theory to Practice

Noor Publishing

Imprint
Any brand names and product names mentioned in this book are subject to trademark, brand or patent protection and are trademarks or registered trademarks of their respective holders. The use of brand names, product names, common names, trade names, product descriptions etc. even without a particular marking in this work is in no way to be construed to mean that such names may be regarded as unrestricted in respect of trademark and brand protection legislation and could thus be used by anyone.

Cover image: www.ingimage.com

Publisher:
Noor Publishing
is a trademark of
International Book Market Service Ltd., member of OmniScriptum Publishing Group
17 Meldrum Street, Beau Bassin 71504, Mauritius

Printed at: see last page
ISBN: 978-620-0-07714-1

Copyright © Hala kh Najim
Copyright © 2020 International Book Market Service Ltd., member of OmniScriptum Publishing Group

Dedication

To My dear Husband Dr.Marwan Tawfiq

       & Sons

          Mohammed, Mustafa

          and lovely daughter

          Safa

Foreword

This book arises directly from my experience in teaching Functional Grammar to Iraqi students at the university level. Functional Grammar is a new trend in English Grammar and a number of students or researchers may be daunted by the new terminology of this approach . The book is an attempt to set out the approach in an easy and accessible way. What I have done is to describe the theoretical and practical background of certain aspects of functional grammar. The author also tries to give a detailed description of Arabic grammar from a functional point of view , and make a sort of comparison between English and Arabic languages. The main aim of this book is to highlight the similarities and differences between English and Arabic from a Systemic Functional Grammar.

The book mainly adopts Michael Halliday`s books – especially his *Introduction to Functional Grammar (1985, 2nd edition 1994, third edition with Christian Matthiessen 2004)*.

HalaKh. Najim (Ph.D)

Contents

Dedication

Chapter One

Systemic Functional Grammar in English

1.<u>What is Systemic Functional Grammar?</u>

According to Matthiessen and Halliday (1997: 3), grammar is the 'system of wordings'. It is one of the subsystems of a language. They claimed that in the history of thinking about language in the west, there have two different theoretical perspectives. In one, language is a set of rules, so grammar is simply a set of rules for identifying the grammatical structures such as the construction of a transitive sentence with verb plus object. Hence, the sentence which is the basic unit is studied in isolation. In the other view, however, language is a resource for creating meanings by means of wording[2]. In this case, the sentence is studied in its discourse environment because the text is considered the basic unit. The first view provides us with a small fragment of language, it does not interpret the whole organization of the grammar of a language as a system of information. Consequently, systemic functional grammar (henceforth SFG) arose. It was first developed in work on the grammar of Chinese; and it has been used in educational and computational contexts. More specifically, SFG deals with grammar as a resource rather than rule, i.e. it takes the resource perspective rather than the rule perspective.

Hudson (1970: 1) argues that SFG is to provide a framework within which the grammar of any natural language can be described. He states:

> **It defines the overall structure that grammars**
> **must have, by defining the kinds of categories**
> **that must appear in them and the way in which**
> **these are related to each other in the grammar;**
> **for instance, according to systemic theory, a**

In SFG, however, the word 'systemic' refers to that feature of the Hallidayan grammar that interprets language not as a set of structures but as a network of systems, or interrelated sets of options for making meaning. Kress (1976: 3) claims that (SFG) is based on the notion of choice. The speaker of a language can be regarded as carrying out simultaneously and successively a number of distinct choices. It is simply the system that formalizes the notion of choice in language. In addition, Crystal (1985: 302) argues that the notion of system is one of four categories recognized by SFG. The others are unit, structure, and class. The various units are considered to be arranged hierachially on a rank scale, and each unit consists of one or more of the units below it. In the later development of this theory, the notion of 'system' is made a central principle, and the language is conceived as a 'system of systems'. SFG accounts for all the semantically relevant choices in the language (ibid.: 302).

In short, Fawcett et al. (1993: 117) point out that the 'choice points' in SFG are called systems, as the first half of the name. As for the second half, it derives from the fact that the features from which choices are made are functional. They add that these choices express meanings of the many types that are needed to mediate the various functions of the language. Thus, what Halliday states is obvious (1994: 15):

> .... it interprets language as a set of structures
> but as a network of systems, or interrelated sets
> of options for making meaning. Such options are
> not defined by reference to structures; they are
> purely abstract features, and structure comes in
> as the means whereby they are put into effect, or
> realized.

In fact, Halliday amongst other systemic linguists, believe that grammar is a way of performing social functions rather than a way of thinking, i.e. they view language as a form of 'doing' rather than as a form of 'knowing'. They, then, give a very high priority to the social aspects of language, while they give a relatively low priority to psychological aspects of language (Berry, 1975: 22f; Butler,1985 266ff)[3].

2. **Elements of the Clause**:

According to SFG, there are four elements of clause structure. They are : S(subject) , P(redicator); C(omplement) and A(djunct). Hence, the structure of a clause from a systemic point of view is SPCA, e.g.

Heisa studentin the college
S P   C   A

Each element is realized by a certain group. S and C, for example, are realized by nominal group (NG), P is realized by verbal group (VG), and A is realized by adverbial group (Muir, 1972: 52f, Berry, 1975: 63).

In contrast to Quirk et al. (1985: 191) who claim that there are obligatory elements in the clause structure, we can say that they are not obligatory but central elements and major clauses. S and P are more central than C and A. In SFG, S is initial, it is the NG which immediately precedes the VG. Also, it is concerned with P (the thing being talked about). It maintains concord with other elements. This means that a NG which has gender bearing pronouns (he, she, it) or one of these pronouns at head, requires the –s form of the verb at P when the tense is not past. Thus, for identifying the S, concord means

3

that a gender bearing VG requires the –s form of the verb (Halliday,1985: 53).

The girl buys the books.

It is 'the girl' which correlates with the –s form of the verb, and since –s form occurs in the clause, 'the girl' is the S of the clause.

As for the NG which operates at the S in the structure, there is a central element which is called the head (h) or head word (ibid.: 25), e.g.

He was pale.
 h

The h element may be preceded by another element which is called modifier (m), which can be realized by a number of words:

a. The boy …
m

b. Thenice boy.
mm

c. Theverynice boy.
m   mm

Also, there is an element of structure which follows the h element but it occurs in the subject position. This is called the qualifier (q):

Boyswith red hair are nice.
 h   q

(Muir, 1972: 26)

The elements m h q could function in subject position as in [The nice boys with red hair are nice].

In addition, Halliday (1994: 25) deals with bracketing which is away of showing what goes with what in what logical order the elements of a linguistic structure are combined. He claims that bracketing does not specify what function the bracketed constituents have in the whole structure. Thus, two types of labelling are distinguished: class labelling and function labelling (ibid.: 27). The former includes classes such as noun, verb, etc.; while the latter refers to functional terms such as subject, object, complement etc. He states:

> **Class labels are, so to speak, part of the dictionary; they indicate the potential that the word, or other item, has in the grammar of the language. Function labels are an interpretation of the text; they indicate the part of the item is playing in the particular structure under consideration.**

Thus, by labelling grammatical functions, we can show what part each component is playing in the overall structure (ibid.: 29). This can be illustrated in figure (1):

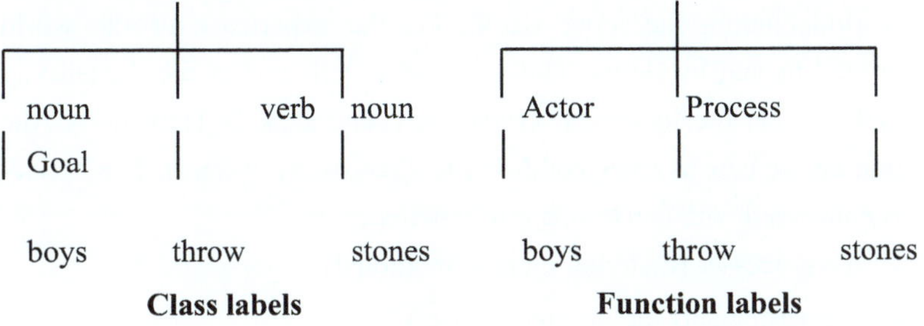

Figure (1): An example of class and function labels.

In addition, Halliday(1994:29) claims that the purpose of functional labelling is to provide a means of interpreting grammatical structure, in such a way as to relate any given instance to the system of the language as a whole .

3. <u>Metafunctions</u> :

According to Halliday (1970: 143), language fulfils three metafunctions: ideational, interpersonal and textual. Metafunctions are distinguished from macrofunctions and microfunctions. Metafunctions are highly generalized functions language has evolved to serve. Macrofunctions, however, refer to language use in early child; and finally, microfunction denote to functionally defined constituents like actor, action, goal (Mattessian and Halliday, 1997: 21). In what follows, we are going to discuss each one of these metafunctions in some detail.

3.1 <u>Ideational metafunction:</u>

It is concerned with the speaker's experience of the real world,including the inner world, i.e. the experience of the world around us and inside us. This function is reflected in the 'transitivity system', i.e. the ideational system at clause rank is Transitivity (the unit clause acts as entry condition to Transitivity system). Transitivity is concerned with construing our experience of:
- the processes (material, mental, relational)
- the participants (actor, goal, carrier)
- circumstances (cause, location, manner)

Hence there is a choice between three types of processes material, mental and relation, e.g.

a. Ali bought a book.

b. Ali saw a bird.

c. Ali is a teacher.

The clause (a) chose the term material process, (b) chose the mental process and (c) chose the relational process.

Halliday also affirms that the experiential meaning is realised in the system of Transitivity within a wide range of choices available in the system of any language. Thus, we use language to represent our experience of the processes, persons, objects, abstractions, and relations of the world around us and inside us (Halliday, 1978: 145).

In addition, Halliday posits that our experiences in the world consist of 'goings-on', that is, a flow of events that represent our outer activities or social manifestations in daily life and our inner thoughts or forms of interpretation of the world. This function of the clause is related to the ideational metafunction. Halliday (1994: 106) describes this by saying:

> **"Language enables human beings to build a mental picture of reality, to make sense of what goes on around them and inside them. Here again, the clause plays a role, because it embodies a general principle for modeling experience – namely, the principle that reality is made up of processes".**

Matthisenand Halliday (1997: 22) argue that the major types of transitivity correspond to three major word classes: verb, noun and adverb. Process, then, is expressed by a verbal group, participants by a nominal group, and circumstances by an adverbial group.

Transitivity is one of the major strands of meaning in the clauses of all human languages. It defines the range of types of process that is possible to be expressed through the language concerned.

Following on the thrust of Halliday's idea, Transitivity system is constituted by the following factors:

(i) Processes in the verbal complex of clauses. The grammar distinguishes between the outer experience, the processes of the external world, and inner experience, the processes of consciousness. The grammatical categories are those of Material Processes and Mental Processes. The third process is to relate one fragment of experience to another. It is called the Relational Process (Halliday, 1994: 107).

(ii) Participants involved in the processes and realised by nominal groups of clauses. The participants can be further described in terms of various participants roles such as Actor, Agent, Goal, Carrier, Sayer, etc.

(iii) Circumstances associated with the processes in adverbial groups or prepositional phrases. Often there will be circumstances attendant on the process, the process happens at some special time or in some special place or for some special reason .

In English grammar, we can make choices between different types of process, between different types of participant, between different types of circumstance and between different numbers of participants and circumstances. These choices are known as the Transitivity system (Berry, 1975: 150). There is a system of three terms: material, mental and relational:

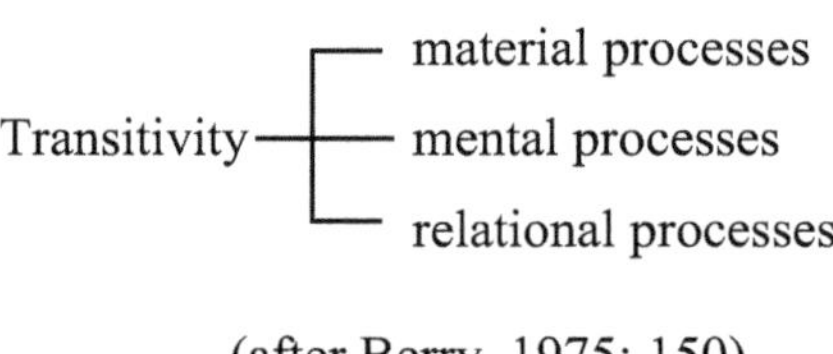

(after Berry, 1975: 150)

Material processes or processes of doing are actions carried out by participants called Agents. They may or may not affect other participants (Halliday and Matthiessen, 2004: 183).

John hit Layla yesterday.

Jack runs.

As shown above, in (1) there are two participants, while in (2) there is only one.

Mental processes, however, are processes of perception (see, hear), of cognition (know, understand), and of affection (like, fear) (Downing and Locke, 2002: 125).

I saw the accident.

He knows the answer.

She likes desserts.

3.2Interpersonalmetafunction:

It is concerned with the interaction between the speaker and addressee(s). Halliday (1970: 143) claims that language establishes social relations which include the communication roles created by language such as the roles of the questioner or the hearer, which we take on by asking or answering a question by means of the interaction between one person and another. Thus, in interacting with one another, we enter into a number of interpersonal relationships, choosing, suggesting, etc. Mood is the system that organizes the various interpersonal relationships among participants in a special environment. In other words, mood systems are choices between different roles which a speaker can select for himself and the hearer. The clause is again the rank of unit which acts as entry condition for the mood system as shown in figure (2):

Entry condition	System name	Terms

Clause	Mood type	indicative
		imperative

Figure (2): A System

Here, the clause chooses between indicative and imperative (Berry, 1977: 166):

a. Has Ali come

b. He is clever.

c. Open the window.

The clauses (a) and (b) chose the indicative, while (c) chose the imperative. Hence, the clauses which chose indicative make a choice between interrogative and declarative. The clauses which chose declarative make another choice between tagged and untagged.

a. He is happy, isn't he?

b. He is happy.

The clause (a) has chosen tagged, while (b) has chosen untagged. However, the clauses which chose interrogative make a further choice between closed interrogative (yes/no) and open interrogative (wh-questions). The speaker of a clause which has chosen yes/no question expects his hearer to say yes or no, whereas that of the clause which has chosen open interrogative expects information(Berry,1975:168):

 a. Do you like coffee?

b. What is your favourite drink?

3.3 Textual metafunction:

Halliday (1970: 143) argues that this metafunction enables the speaker or writer to construct 'texts' or connected passages of discourse that is relevant; and enables the listener or the reader to distinguish a text from a random set of sentences. That is, language provides means for making links with itself and the situational context in which it is used. This textual metafunction provides resources for presenting interpersonal and ideational meanings as information organized into text that can be exchanged between the speaker and the hearer (Matthissen and Halliday, 1997: 22). At clause rank, the textual system is Theme. Thus, Theme is a resource for organizing the interpersonal and ideational meanings of each clause in the form of a message. In English, theme is realized by initial position and Rheme is realized by non-initial position, e.g.

a.<u>Ali</u> is a football player.
  Theme

We may distinguish between two types of clauses: those unmarked for theme, and those marked for theme (Muir, 1972: 98). A declarative clause, for example, in which the subject element (S) in initial position is unmarked for theme (see a.). However, in English, the marked theme may occur in different positions of the elements of the clause. The complement (C) may occur in clause-initial position.

Football I'll play anytime.

We know that the normal order of the English clause is SPC, i.e. the C in clause structure follows P. But in (5), the clause has marked theme which is termed (thematic C), marked by initial position of C.

Similarly, the clause may be marked for theme by the initial position of adjunct A (A-theme), e.g.

a. On Friday I'm going to the cinema.

b. On the shore Peter cut his foot.

(Berry, 1975: 164)

Thus, this distinction shows in the surface structure, since a clause which has chosen unmarked theme will have S initially, while a clause which has chosen marked theme will have, P, C or A in first place (ibid.: 163).

$$\longrightarrow \left[\begin{array}{l} \text{unmarked} \\ \text{marked} \end{array} \right.$$

Kress, (1976: 29), however, claims that these three metafunctions of language are manifested in the grammatical structure. In English, the clause is a realization of meaning derived from the ideational, interpersonal and textual metafunctions. Thus, all these components are embodied at the same time. Let us consider the following:

-The sun was shining on the sea.

(Kress, 1976: 29)

This clause shows these three metafunctions of grammatical structures:

	the sun	was shining	on the sea
experiential	Affected	Process	Locative
Interpersonal	Modal		Propositional
Textual	Theme		Rheme

Figure (3): Three dimensions of the grammatical structure of the clause

4. **Subject, Actor,Theme :**

Halliday(1994:30) argues that linguistic items are multifunctional, i.e. a constituent has more than one function at a time. The subject, then, is considered a multifunctional item. In the above figure (3), for example, the item 'boys' is labelled actor, but it functions as subject and theme at the same time. In fact, Halliday ascribes to the subject notion a number of different functions depending on three broad definitions, which are obviously not synonymous . They could be summarized as follows:

(i)   that which is the concern of the message.

(ii)   that of which something is being predicted.

(iii)   the doer of the action.

Let us consider, now, the following clause:

-<u>The duke</u> gave my aunt this teapot.

(ibid.: 30)

In 'the duke" is the subject in all these three definitions. He is the one with whom the message is concerned; the truth or falsehood of the statement is vested in him; and he has done the action of giving. Thus, the roles or functions of theme, subject and actor are all combined or conflated in 'the duke'. This is illustrated in the following figure:

the duke	gave my aunt this teapot
Theme subject actor	

Figure (4): An element functioning as theme, subject and actor.

13

These three definitions are later equated with psychological subject, grammatical subject, and logical subject respectively (Halliday,1994: 31):

(i)   **Psychological subject**: It meant the concern of the message. It was called 'psychological' because it was what the speaker had in his mind to start with, when embarking on the production of the clause.

(ii)   **Grammatical subject**: 'that of which something is predicted'. It was called 'grammatical' because at that time the construction of subject and predicate was thought of as a purely formal grammatical relationship. That is, there is concord of person and number with the verb, but it was not thought to express any particular meaning.

(iii)   **Logical subject**: It meant the 'doer of the action'. It was called 'logical' in the sense that of 'having to do with relations between things', as opposed to grammatical relations, which are relations between symbols (ibid.: 31).

However, Halliday (1994: 32) replaces the earlier labels by separate ones which relate more specifically to the functions concerned:

psychological subject: theme

grammatical subject: subject

logical subject: actor

Thus, figure (5) can be relabelled as in:

the duke	gave my aunt this teapot
psychological subject	

grammatical subject logical subject	

Figure (5): An element functioning as psychological, grammatical and logical subject.

It should be noticed that all these three functions are conflated at one time in the above-mentioned example. However, not all English clauses contain such element that embodies all these three. For example:

- This teapot my aunt was given by the duke.

The duke, here, is still the actor; but the message is concerned with this teapot (theme), and the truth of the message is vested in my aunt (S.). So, the psychological, grammatical and logical subject are realized by different items. This can be shown in the following figure:

This teapot	my aunt	was given by	the duke
Theme psychological S.	Subject grammatical S.		Actor logical S.

Figure (6): Different terms realize psychological, grammatical and logical subject.

In other words, the psychological S. is 'this teapot' (the concern of the message). The grammatical S., however, is 'my aunt' who is the one of whom the statement is predicated, and can be argued about as true or false. Only 'the duke' is still the logical S. Hence in figure(5), the roles of Theme, Subject and Actor are all combined, while in figure(6), they are separated:

Furthermore, Halliday (1994: 33) gives different conflations of these roles:

-<u>My aunt</u> was given this teapot by <u>the duke</u>.
Theme/Subject   Actor

-<u>This teapotthe duke</u> gave to my aunt.
        Theme   Actor/Subject

-<u>The dukemy aunt</u> was given this teapot.
  Actor/Theme/ Subject

Finally, Halliday claims that these different conflations of the subject make up a separable strand in the whole meaning of the clause. He determines these functions in the clause as follows (ibid.: 34):

(i)   The theme functions in the structure of the clause AS A MESSAGE.

(ii)   The subject functions in the structure of the clause AS AN EXCHANGE.

(iii)   The actor functions in the structure of the clause AS A REPRESENTATION.

These three different interpretations of the clause will be described in the following sections:

5.<u>Clause As a Message:</u>

According to Halliday, the clause, in textual metafunction, is organized as a message. It has a structure known as a 'thematic structure' which gives the clause its character, i.e. as a message (Halliday, 1970: 161; 1985: 38). The English clause consists of Theme and Rheme (written with an initial capital). The Theme is another component in the complex notion of subject, namely the 'psychological subject.Itis the starting point for the message (Halliday, 1967: 212). It can be defined as that element which comes in the first position in the clause (Kress, 1976: 180). It is normal in English for the element selected as "theme" to be the subject of the sentence (Hutchins, 1975: 101). Matthisen and Halliday (1997: 22) define Theme as a resource for organizing the interpersonal and ideational meanings of each clause in the form of a message. A message, then, consists of Theme accompanied by Rheme which is the part in which Theme is developed. Let us consider the following:

a.The duke (has given my aunt this teapot).

      Theme   Rheme

b.My aunt (has been given this teapot).

      Theme   Rheme

In the above examples, the Themes of the clauses are the elements which are put in subject positions normally realized by NGs, while what are inside the brackets being Rhemes.

The structure of the clause is divided into two parts: Theme and Rheme. Theme is the point of departure of the clause as a message. It functions as the 'starting point for the message' (Halliday, 1985: 39), the element which the clause is going to be 'about' has a crucial effect in orienting listeners and readers. Theme is one element in a particular structural configuration which, taken as a whole, organizes the clause as a message; this is the configuration Theme + Rheme. In other words, a message consists of a Theme combined with a Rheme (Halliday, 1994: 38). Theme is the starting point of the clause, realisedby whatever element comes first and Rheme is the rest of the message, which provides the additional information added to the starting point and which is available for the subsequent development in the text.The clause as a message is thus a configuration of two thematic status, Theme + Rheme (Halliday, 1994: 38).

Matthiessen and Halliday (1997: 17) argue that at the clause rank, the major textual system is Theme. The system of Theme sets up a local environment, providing a point of departure by reference to which the listener interprets the message. The local environment, serving as a point of departure, is the Theme; what is presented in this local environment is the Rheme.

In English, Theme is realised by an initial position and Rheme is realised by a non-initial position (ibid., 1997: 17). For this reason, in a declarative structure (John read an interesting story yesterday), [John] is (theme) and [read an interesting story yesterday] is (Rheme). The different choice of Theme has contributed to a different meaning and English uses first clausal position as a signal to orient a different meaning of the sentence. Thus, in [An interesting story, John read yesterday] and [Yesterday, John read an interesting story], we start the message from a different point, i.e., to choose a different theme for the clause. As Halliday (1994: 38) mentioned, Theme is the ground from which the clause is taking off. What makes [An interesting story, John read yesterday] and [Yesterday, John read an interesting story] is that they differ in their choice of Theme and they tell us what an interesting story, and what yesterday is going to be about.

Downing and Locke (2002: 223) state that the choice of Theme is important because it represents the angle from which the speaker projects his/her message. The initial element acts as a signal to the hearer, directing expectations regarding the structure that is likely to follow, or about the mental representation of what the message is likely to be. Thus, a Theme which coincides with the subject prepares the hearer for a declarative structure (He can speak English), while presentative 'there' introduces new information to the hearer (There was an accident).

In addition, the choice of the initial element concerns the speaker's assumptions regarding what the hearer knows or does not know (ibid.). Let us consider:

a.I can't stand the noise.
b.The noise I can't stand.
c.It's the noise I can't stand.
d.What I can't stand is the noise.

(Downing and Locke, 2002: 223)

In (a), no particular supposition is made about the situation on the part of the hearer, apart from the definiteness of the noise. The second clause implies a contrast with something else (though the people are friendly). In (c), the speaker presupposes a shared belief with the hearer that I can't stand something. The fourth clause, however, restricts what the speaker can't stand among other things imagined by the hearer.

5.1 Unmarked and Marked Theme:

Halliday (1994: 43) claims that major clauses have thematic structures, while minor clauses have not. The major clauses are indicative or imperative in mood; if indicative, there is a choice between declarative or interrogative; if interrogative, there is a choice between polar interrogative (yes/no questions) or wh-questions.

Theme is a meaningful choice and speakers can choose between marked and an unmarked option (Dowing and Lock, 2002: 226).

The unmarked Theme is the subject in a declarative clause, the wh-word in a wh-interrogative clause and the finite verbal element in a polar interrogative (Kress, 1976: 180). In declarative clauses, the subject is chosen as unmarked Theme. However, the marked Theme in the declarative clauses is the Theme which is something other than the subject. In other words, the usual marked Theme is an adverbial group or prepositional phrase. Also, the complement can be the marked Theme in the declarative clauses (Berry, 1975: 164). Let's analyze the following examples to markedness:

-Merrily we roll along.
-Adverbial group
(marked Theme)

-On Saturday night I lost my wife.
 Prepositional phrase
 (marked Theme)
-Nature in nature I loved.
  Complement

  (marked Theme)

As shown above, the Themes are all marked because they are adverbial group, prepositional phrase and complements respectively. Strictly speaking, there are some reasons behind using marked Themes (as quoted in Farhan, 1999: 24).

(1) Setting the stage for later information, e.g.

Th   Rh

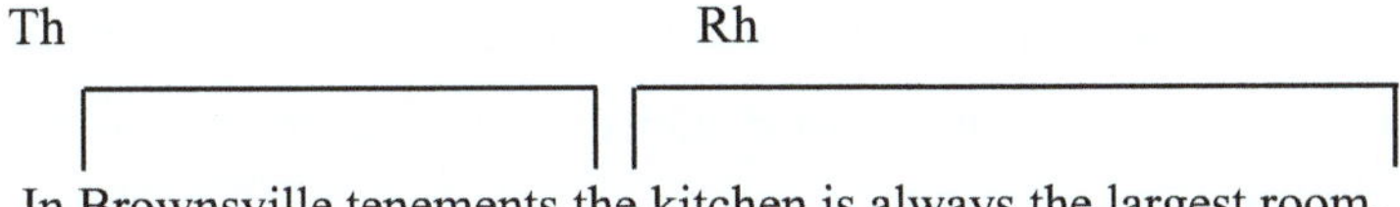

In Brownsville tenements the kitchen is always the largest room.

(2) Calling attention to bits of information or to invest them with a

highly charged quality:

Th   Rh

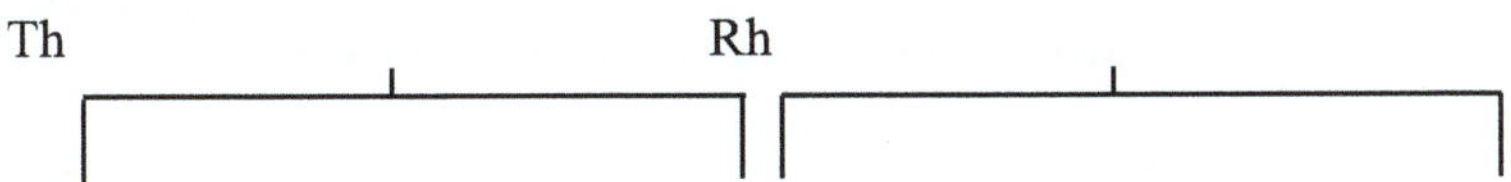

This resorting to psychological denial they do where nuclear war is concerned.

(Galbraith, 1988: 310)

(3) To show contrast:

(Kopple, 1991: 321)

Hence, we can say that the clause which has chosen unmarked Theme will have the element in the first place, while the clause which has chosen marked Theme will have P, C or A at the beginning (Berry, 1975: 163).

As for the English interrogative clauses, they are of two main types: Polarity 'yes or no' and wh-questions. In the first type, the element that functions as unmarked Theme is the finite verbal operator because it is the finite operator that expresses positive or negative. Here, the Theme extends over the subject. In fact, there are a two-part Theme which consists of the operator plus subject as illustrated below:

Can	you	believe him ?
Is	he	alive ?
Th (1)	Th (2)	Rh

Figure (7): Theme in yes/no interrogative.

However, in the wh-question, the element which is considered Theme is the wh-word that requests this information, it is the wh-element that expresses the nature of the missing piece (Halliday, 1994: 46):

Who	are you?
What	is he doing now?
Theme	Rheme

Figure (8): Theme is wh-interrogative.

In both types, the choice of unmarked thematic pattern is motivated. That is, there is a strong tendency for the speaker to choose the unmarked form and not to reduce a marked Theme. The marked Themes in interrogative clauses occur when complements or adverbial groups are fronted. This can be shown in the following example:

After tea	will you visit me?
Theme	Rheme

Figure (9): Marked Theme in an interrogative clause.

To sum up, one distinction drawn by Halliday is between unmarked and marked Theme in relation to mood system. It was found that the unmarked Theme is the subject in declarative clauses, the operator and the immediately following words in polar interrogatives and the wh-words in content interrogatives. Thus, if an element other than the subject of the declarative clause is fronted, the Theme is said to be marked.

5.1.2 <u>Simpleand Multiple Themes:</u>

The Theme of a clause is simple when it consists of one structural element, and that element could be represented by only one unit single nominal group, adverbial group or prepositional phrase as in:

a.<u>Very carefullyshe cleaned the house.</u>

       Theme   Rheme

b.<u>With sobs and tearsshe left him.</u>

         Theme   Rheme

However, the Theme may consist of two or more groups or phrases. Such groups or phrases are termed group complex or phrase complex functioning as a Theme. Such Themes are still within the category of 'simple Themes':

a. Ahmed and Ali are here.

b. From town to town he chased him.

As illustrated above, any group complex, for example (a), the two NGs joined by 'and' make up a NG complex. It is one element in the clause and therefore forms a simple Theme. In (b), the two prepositional phrases 'from town to town' likewise constitute a prepositional phrase complex, and this is also considered one simple Theme (Halliday, 1994: 40).

Also, there are simple Themes whereby two or more separate elements are grouped so that they form a single constituent in the structure of the clause. Such case is called a Thematic Equative because it sets up the Theme + Rheme in the form of an equation, e.g.

a. What the duke gave to my aunt/ (Theme)

/was that teapot (Rheme)

b. The one who gave my aunt that teapot/ (Theme)

/was the duke (Rheme)

(ibid.: 41)

In the thematic equatives, all the elements of the clause are organized into two constituents; these two are linked by a relationship of identity, expressed by the verb be. In formal grammar, they are called pseudo-cleft sentences. They realize two semantic features, on the one hand it specifies what the Theme is, on the other hand, it equates it with the Rheme (halliday,1994: 41). Also, they are known as nominalization, whereby any element or group of elements function as NG in the clause as Theme. But nominalization may be the Rheme, in which the Thematic equative becomes marked, e.g.

<u>-This bookis what I gave to Layla</u>

    Theme   Rheme

In the typical instance the nominalization functions as the theme. But in contrast with the typical structure as exemplified by the above example, there is a marked Thematic equative with 'this book' as

Theme and the nominalization becomes the Rheme. For further examples, see the following:

a. <u>Thatis the one I like</u>.
ThemeRheme
b.<u>A loaf of breadis what we chiefly need</u>.
     Theme   Rheme

However, a Theme may combine three types of meanings usually referred to as the above-mentioned metafunctions, and we use for them the terms ideational, interpersonal and textual. Such a case is called Multiple Themes. The internal structure of multiple Theme is based on the principle that a clause is the product of three simultaneous semantic processes. It is a representation of experience, an interactive exchange and a message at the same time (Halliday, 1985: 53). In other words, the multiple Theme has three components: textual Theme, interpersonal Theme, and experiential Theme (ideational or topical) Theme. So, a Theme which has, besides the ideational elements, one or more elements expressing interpersonal and/or textual meanings is called a multiple Theme (ibid.: 53).

The Ideational Theme refers to the representation of "our experience of the world that lies about us, and also inside us, the world of our imagination. It is meaning in the sense of content" (ibid.: 53). The ideational meaning represents 'processes': actions, events, mental processes and relations. Significantly, the subject (S) is the ideational element in the declarative clause; we shall refer to this as Topical Theme, because it corresponds to the element identified as 'topic' in topic-comment analysis. Later on, Halliday (1994) adopts the Experiential Theme.

As for the Textual theme, it is any combination of:

(a) Continuatives (words such as yes, no, well, oh).

(b) Conjunctions such as the coordinators (and, or), the subordinators (when, while, until), and relatives whether they are definite as (which, who, whose, where), or indefinite as (whatever, whoever, whenever).

(c) Conjunctive adjuncts (words such as that is, in other words, also, therefore, etc.).

So, Halliday (ibid.: 54) argues that if one or more of these words appear, they precede the Topical Theme e.g.

(Olson, 1966: 35 as quoted in Farhan, 1999: 26)

However, the Interpersonal Theme is a combination of (a) vocative (b) a modal Theme which is any of the modal adjuncts (such as probably, certainly, etc.); and (c) mood-marking Theme which is either a finite verbal operator or a wh-interrogative. Let us consider the following:

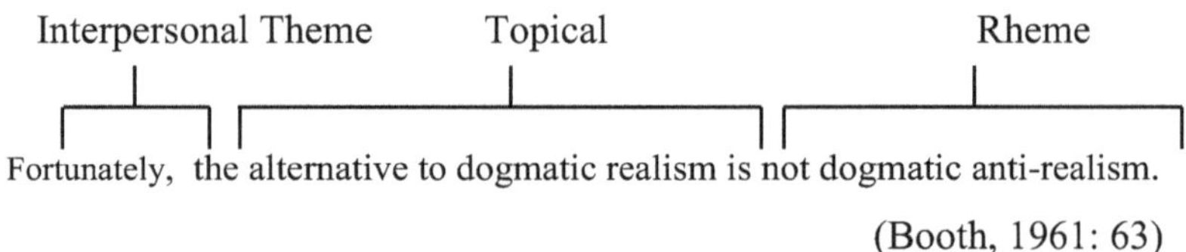

(Booth, 1961: 63)

Another example is given in figure (10):

Girls and boys,	come out	to play
Vocative	topical	
Interpersonal		Rheme
Theme		

Figure (10): An example of multiple Theme.

(Halliday, 1985: 55)

It should be clarified, here, that these two components of Theme, i.e. Textual and Interpersonal, normally precede the Topical or Experiential Theme. The typical order of the multiple Theme is: Textual-Interpersonal-Topical. The Topical Theme, then, comes last, so "whatever follows the first ideational element of the clause is automatically part of the Rheme" (Halliday,1994: 53):

Oh	soldier, soldier	won't	you	marry me
continuative	vocative	finite	topical	
textual	interpersonal		experiential	Rheme
Theme				

Figure (11): A further example of multiple Theme.

6.Clause as Exchange:

Clause as an exchange corresponds to the interpersonal metafunction. In interacting with one another, we engage into a range of interpersonal relationships such as ordinary, asking, etc. Halliday(1970: 159) claims that one function of language is to provide for interaction between people. He goes to say that:

> **language itself defines the roles which people may take in situations in which they are communicating with one another, and every**

This metafunction is called interpersonal metafunction. The clause, here, is organized as an interactive event between the speaker and the hearer. Two types of speech roles are distinguished: giving and demanding, the speaker gives a piece of information to the hearer or he demands something from him. Thus, it can be considered as an exchange as 'giving' which implies receiving and 'demanding' which implies giving in response (Halliday, 1994: 68). Consequently, the act of giving and demanding can be referred to two types of exchange, namely exchange of good and services (offers and commands) and exchange information (statement and question).

Halliday (1994:68) draws a distinction between giving and demanding of information and goods and services. In the case of an exchange of goods and services, the exchange of commodity is usually non-verbal, i.e. what is being demanded is an object or action. However, in the exchange of information, the speaker says something to the hearer with the aim of getting a piece of information. What is being demanded, here, is information, i.e. the response is a verbal one. Thus, language is the end as well as the means.

6.1 <u>Mood:</u>

The system of the clause as exchange is Mood. The mood systems are simply choices between different roles of the speaker and the hearer (Berry, 1975: 166).It organizes the various interpersonal relationships among participants (Matthissenand Halliday, 1997: 14). In questions, for example, the speaker takes the role of seeking information and requires the listener to take on the role of giving the information (Halliday, 1994: 68). The clause chooses between indicative and imperative. The speaker of a clause which has chosen imperative has selected for himself the role of controller and that of controlled for his hearer. The speaker of a clause which has chosen indicative, however, has not selected any of the above mentioned roles. In such a case, the speaker expects a verbal response from his hearer. Thus, the clause 'Has Ali come?' has chosen the indicative, while 'Open the door' has chosen the imperative. In SFG, this can be shown as:

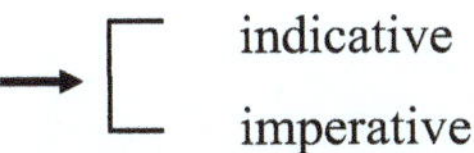

Furthermore, the clause which has chosen indicative make a choice between interrogative and declarative. The speaker of a declarative clause has selected for himself the information role, while the speaker of a clause which has chosen the interrogative has selected the role of informed and for his hearer the informant, e.g.

a.They hung the pictures.

b. Did they hang the picture?

Also, the clauses which have chosen declarative make a choice between tagged and untagged. For example, [He is happy, isn't he?] has chosen tagged, while [he is happy] has chosen untagged. However, the clause which has chosen interrogative makes a further choice between closed interrogation (yes/no) and open interrogation. Thus, [Has he come?] chooses closed interrogation, while [Why did you come?] chooses open interrogation.

As for the imperative clauses, they make choices between exclusive imperatives and inclusive imperatives. The speaker who has chosen exclusive imperative excludes himself from the action, while that who has chosen inclusive includes himself, e.g.

a. Open the door. (exclusive)

b. Let's go for a walk. (inclusive)

These choices are illustrated in the following figure:

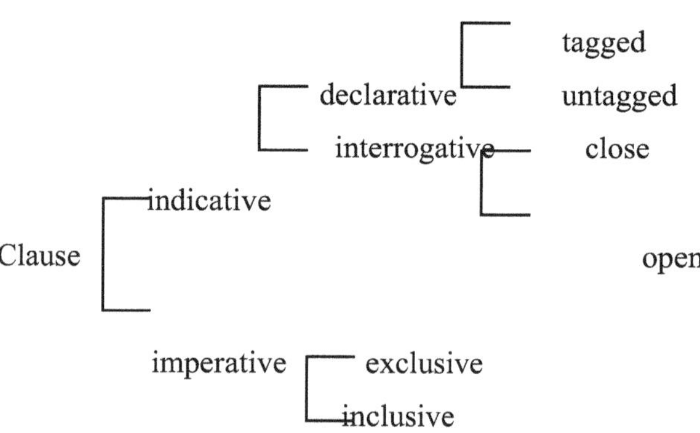

Figure (12): Mood system after Berry (1975: 160ff)

The mood consists of two parts: the subject which is a nominal group and the finite operator which is part of the verbal group (Halliday, 1994: 72). Subject and finite, they are combined forming one constituent which is called mood. The grammatical relation of these

30

two elements of the mood determine whether the clause is a statement or a question.

In a declarative clause, the subject is that element which can be recognized by the pronoun in the tag. For example:

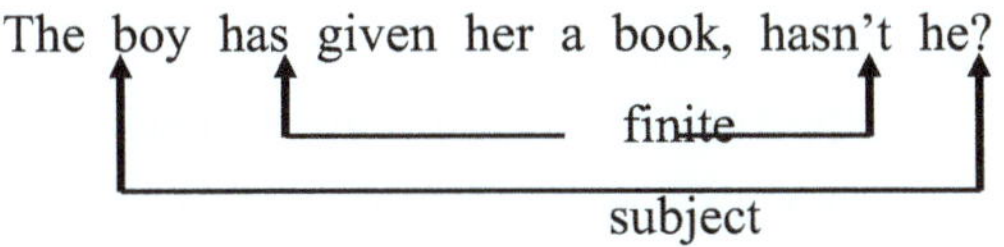

So, in order to pick up the subject in the above example, we add a tag and see which element is recognized. In the tag 'hasn't he', 'he' is a replacement for the grammatical subject which is 'the boy'. We can say, then, that the grammatical subject is the nominal group that is repeated in a pronoun form in the tag in every declarative clause.

Halliday (1994: 72) claims that the label 'grammatical subject' implies a grammatical function whose only function is grammatical, whereas the subject in question is semantic in origin.

Subject then is identified as that noun or pronoun that is in person and number concord with the verb. In English the mood consists of subject which is a nominal group and the finite operator which is part of a verbal group, for example, in [He will come soon], 'he' is the subject and 'will' is the finite. The finite element is, then, one of the verbal operators which express tense or modality. It should be noted that the finite element and the lexical verb are fused into a single word, e.g. loves. This happens when the verb is simple past or simple present, active voice (ibid.).

This leads us to say that the subject and finite are combined to form what is called the Mood. So, the Mood is the element that realizes the selection of mood in the clause. The meaning of the subject supplies the rest of what it takes to form a proposition, something to which the proposition can be affirmed or denied, for example, in [Jack has sent me a letter], 'Jack' specifies the person in respect of which the assertion is affirmed. In other words, it is 'Jack' in whom the achievement or failure of the proposition is vested. Thus, Jack is the one who is responsible for the functioning of the clause as an interactive action.

It is the subject that specifies the responsible element, while in a proposition this means the one on which the validity of the information is made .

However, the function of the finite element is to make the proposition finite. That is, it makes the proposition something that can be argued about, i.e. it relates the proposition to its context in the speech event. This is achieved by means of two ways. One is by reference to the time of speaking, e.g. 'was' in [Ali was writing a letter]. The other is by reference to the judgement of the speaker, e.g. 'can't' in [It can't be true].

Strictly speaking, the first is <u>primary tense</u>, the second is <u>modality</u>. What is meant by primary tense is past, present at the moment of speaking. On the other hand, modality means the speaker's judgement of the probabilities or the obligations. Hence, finiteness is expressed by means of a verbal operator which is either temporal or modal. Also, there is another feature to finiteness which is polarity, i.e. the choice between positive and negative. So, the finite element expresses primary tense or modality, and also realizes a polarity feature.

A part from the subject and the finite, the rest of the clause is called the Residue. It consists of the predicator (P), complement (C), and adjunct (A). Hence, the clause as an exchange can be analysed in terms of SFPCA. On the other hand, the subject provides what the clause states or asks. It is the order of the subject and finite that defines

the mood of the clause which can be indicative or imperative
Halliday(1994:72) argues:

> **the characteristic expression of a statement is the declarative, that of a question is the interrogative, and within the category of interrogative, there is a further distinction between yes-no interrogative, for polar questions, and wh-interrogative, for content questions.**

The grammatical category that is characteristically used to exchange information is the indicative; within the category of indicative.

These features are described below:

1. The presence of the mood element, consisting of subject and finite, realizes the feature indicative.
2. In the indicative, the order of subject and finite is significant:

(a)   the subject before finite realizes 'declarative'.

(b)   the finite before the subject realizes 'yes-no' question.

(c)   In wh-questions, the order is:

(i)   subject before finite of the wh-element is the subject.

(ii)   Finite before subject in others. Consider:

a. The girl has bought a book. (indicative)

b. Has the girl bought a book? (yes-no interrogative)

In (a), the mood indicates a declarative choice, while the mood in (b) shows an interrogative choice. The structure of these examples are illustrated in figures below:

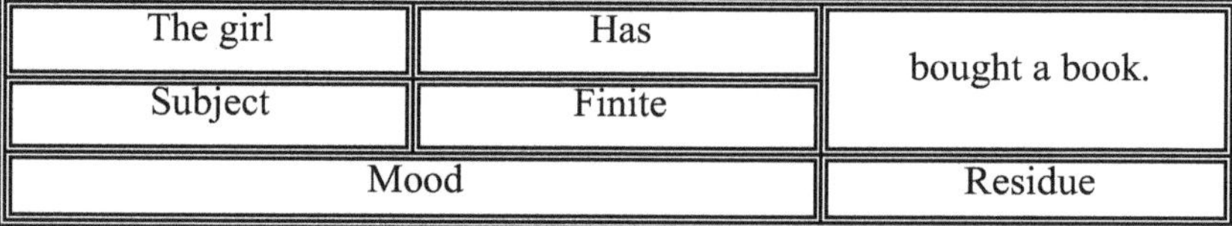

The girl	Has	bought a book.
Subject	Finite	
Mood		Residue

Figure (13): A structure of declarative.

Has	the girl	bought a book?
Finite	Subject	
Mood		Residue

Figure (14): A structure of yes/no questions.

In (a), the subject is 'the girl' and the finite is 'has'; and the structure of the mood is SF, which indicates a declarative mood. In (b), however, the finite 'has' precedes the subject which is typical of the interrogative mood in English.

As for the meaning of subject, it supplies the rest of the propsoition. It specifies the entity in respect of which the assertion has validity. For example, in (a) above, it is the subject in whom the success or failure of the proposition is vested. Here, the finite 'has' refers to positive polarity and present time.

7.Clause as Representation:

The grammatical subject is dealt with at the clause from the viewpoint of its interpersonal metafunction, i.e. the clause as an exchange (the part the clause plays as an exchange between the speaker and the hearer). However, in this section, the clause in its experiential or ideational metafunction is discussed. Halliday (1994: 106) described this as follows:

> **language enables human beings to build a mental
> picture of reality, to make sense of what goes on
> around them and inside them. Here again the clause
> plays a central role, because it embodies a general
> principle for modelling experience – namely, the
> principle that reality is made up of PROCESSES.**

In other words, language serves for the expression of 'content', i.e. the speaker's experience of the real world, including the inner world of his own consciousness (Halliday, 1970: 143). This metafunction is called ideational or experiential metafunction. It engenders resources for construing our experience of the world around us and inside us (Matthissen and Halliday, 1997: 12). The ideational system at clause rank is Transitivity. In fact, two types of experience are distinguished: (a) types of process which are related to the outer experience of what is going on in the world outside us and (b) types of participants which are concerned with the inner experience which is a kind of reaction to the external world. In principle, Halliday (ibid.: 107) states that a process is made up of three components:

(i)   the process itself.

(ii)   Participants in the process;

(iii)   circumstances related to the process.

Consequently, in the following example:

The child slept in the room.

'the child' is a participants, 'slept' is the process, and 'in the room' is a circumstantial element.

Typically, the process is realized by a verbal group, the participant is realized by a nominal group; and the circumstance by an adverbial group or prepositional phrase. Thus, the above example can be illustrated in figure (15):

The child	slept	in the room
Participant	process	Circumstance
NG	VG	Prepositional phrase

Figure (15): A clause as process, participant and circumstance.

7.1 Processes Types:

7.1.1 Material Processes: Process of Doing:

A material process construes doings as happenings of actions, activities and events. In English, the material clauses refer to processes in which there is an obligatory actor and optional goal. In other words, in this type of process, the subject is called an <u>Actor</u> with or without a second participant which is called a Goal (Halliday,1994: 110):

The birds	Fly
Actor	Process

Figure (16): A one-participant clause.

The girl	Broke	the window
Actor	Process	Goal

Figure (17): A two-participant clause.

According to Halliday, the material processes are termed processes of doing because there is an entity which does something to another and can be replaced by the verb 'do', for example:

- What did John do?

-He ran away. What John did was run away

(Halliday, 1994: 117)

Also, the material processes are termed processes of happening; so we can ask what happened to John? instead of what did John do?

Material processes, however, may be either concrete physical events (as in the above mentioned examples or abstract doings and happenings as in:

The chairman	Resigned
Actor	Process

Figure (18): A clause with abstract process.

7.1.2 <u>Mental Processes: Processes of Sensing:</u>

Mental processes refer to the clauses of sensing, cognition, perception, feeling, and thinking, e.g.

a. No one believed his story.

b. I hadn't noticed that.

(Halliday,1994: 114)

Unlike the material processes in which the subject is called the Actor, in the mental processes, the subject is the participant who feels, senses and thinks, i.e. the participant who is endowed with consciousness. It is called a Sensor who is the conscious being who feels or thinks, normally realized by NG, while the rest of the clause is referred to as Phenomenon which is felt, thought or sensed. This can be shown below:

John	Believes	Me
Senser	Process	Phenomenon

She	doesn't like	Him
Senser	Process	Phenomenon

Figure (19): Clauses with mental processes.

Mental processes differ from material processes in that in the former the participant (Senser) is required to be human. Thus, we can say (Halliday,1994: 115):

a.Layla knows the answer, but we cannot say.

***b.** The cat knows the answer.

Also, the mental processes cannot be substituted by 'do', which is not the case with material clauses. In mental processes, for example, we do not say:

* What Layla did was know the answer.

Another distinction between mental and material processes is that the material processes fall into two types: intransitive (with one participant 'Actor') and transitive (with two participants 'Actor' and 'Goal'). However, all mental processes involve a Senser and a Phenomenon. This does not imply that these two elements should be present in the clauses, e.g.

(a) Jack cannot see.

Although the phenomenon in (a) is not present, it is implicitly expressed, i.e. Jack cannot see the picture, the person, or perhaps he lost his eyesight. That is, there is presumably something which is not made explicit (ibid.).

Within the category of mental process, there are subtypes which are:

(1) perception such as feel, see, hear, note, etc.

(2) affection such as like, fear, worry, scare, hurt, etc.

(3) cognition such as think, know, believe, puzzle, understand, etc.

Examples in figure (20) (ibid.: 118):

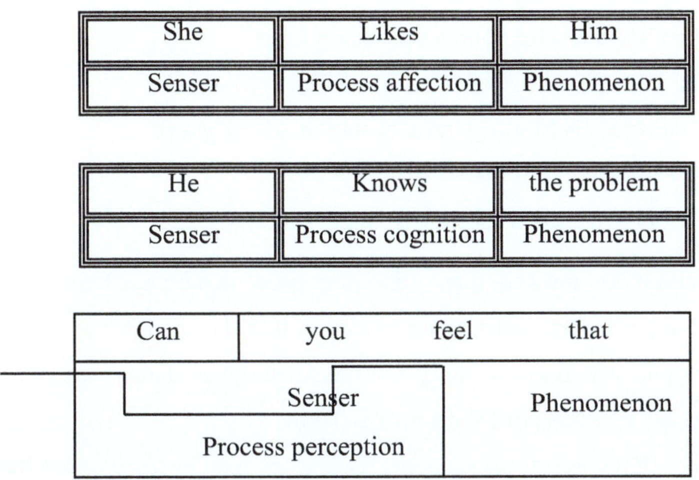

Figure (20): Examples of mental process

7.1.3 <u>Relational Processes: Processes of Being:</u>

A third process type is that of relational processes or processes of being. In relational clauses, there are two parts to the 'being'. That is, a relation is being set up between two entities. In English, there are three main types of relational processes: intensive, circumstantial and possessive. These types can be clarified as follows:

1. intensive X is a

2. circumstantial X is at a

3. possessive X has a

(Halliday,1994: 119)

Each of these has two modes: attributive (a is an attribute of X) and identifying (a is the identity of X). The following examples illustrate these types:

a. John is clever. (intensive attributive)

b. Tom is the teacher. (intensive identifying)

c. The match is on Friday. (circumstantial attributive)

d. Tomorrow is Monday. (circumstantial identifying)

e. Jack has a book. (possessive attribute)

f. The book is Jack's. (possessive identifying)

It should be noticed, here, that the main difference between the attributive and the identifying modes is that the identifying ones are reversible which is not the case with attributive. Hence, we can say [Tom is the leader] or [The leader is Tom].

In the following sections, these types will be discussed in some detail.

7.1.3.1 Intensive Processes: Attributive:

In the intensive attributive processes, an entity has some quality attributed to it. In such clauses, the subject element is called the Carrier that is the entity to which the quality is attributed or ascribed, while this quality is termed the attributive which is indefinite. This can be interpreted as 'x is a member of the class of a'. Thus, when we say [She is clever] 'clever' is the name of a class; consequently, 'She' is a member of the class of clever ones. That is, 'She' is a member of the class of people who are clever. This characteristic specifies one of her attributes; but it does not identify her. Another example is given in figure (21):

A

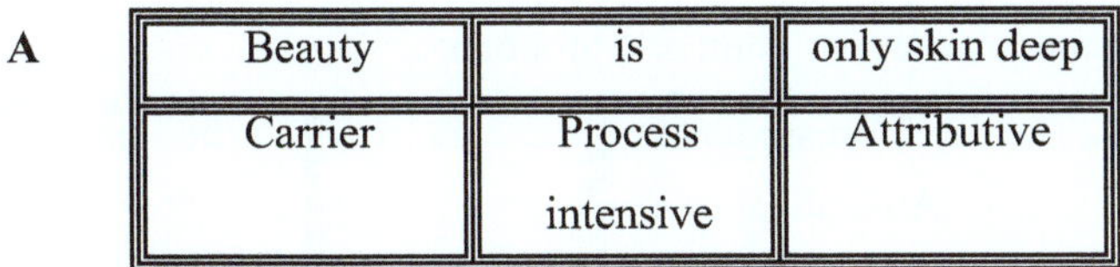

Beauty	is	only skin deep
Carrier	Process intensive	Attributive

Figure (21): An example of intensive attributive clause.

(Berry, 1975: 151)

These clauses are not reversible in the sense that they are systematically agnate forms. Thus, (a) is not reversible, i.e. there is not a sentence like 'only skin deep is beauty' which is agnate to 'Beauty is only skin deep'.

7.1.3.2 Intensive Processes: Identifying:

In intensive identifying processes, one entity is used to identify another: 'x is identified by a' or 'a identifies x'. The subject element is labelled Identified, while the complement is the Identifier (Halliday, 1994: 123):

Ali	is	the captain
Identified	Process	Identifier

Figure (22): An example of intensive identifying clause.

The significant difference between these clauses and the attributive ones is that the former are reversible, so that x-element and a-element can be substituted. 'Ali is the captain', for example, can be replaced by 'The captain is Ali'.

Another distinction between these clauses and the attributive is that the subject element (NG) is definite; it normally has a common noun as head, or a proper noun or a pronoun:

C	The deadliest spiders in Australia They	are	the funnel webs
	Identified	Process intensive	Identifier

Figure (23): Another example of intensive identifying clause
(after Halliday, 1994: 123)

7.1.4 <u>Behavioural Processes:</u>

In the previous section, we have dealt with the basic type of process in the English clause. However, there are subsidiary process types which are behavioural and verbal. Behavioural processes share the characteristics of material and mental process types. That is, they are partially like the material and partially like the mental (Halliday,1994: 139). They are processes of psychological behaviours. The subject who is behaving is termed 'BEHAVER" (typically human).

There are five typical types of behavioural process. They are as follows:

1. Processes of consciousness as forms of behaviour such as look, watch. worry, think (near mental).

2. Verbal processes as behaviour, e.g. chatter, talk, (near verbal).

3. Psychological processes, e.g. laugh, smile, frown.

4. Other psychological processes, e.g. breathe, cough, sleep.

5. Bodily postures, e.g. sing, dance (near material)

Hence, the grammatical function of the subjectis 'Behaver'. See the figure below.

A			
	She	sang	a song
	He	slept	
	The child	laughs	
	Behaver	Process	Matter

Figure (24): Examples of behavioural processes.

7.1.5 Verbal Process:

These are processes of saying which share the character of mental and relational. The grammatical function of the subject is termed 'Sayer'. Functionally, what is said functions as the secondary clause in the clause complex which is either (a) directly quoted or (b) indirectly reported (Halliday,1994: 140). In other words, the first clause in (a) is 'quoting' while the second is 'quoted'. However, in (b), the first clause is 'reporting', and the second is 'reported'. Figure (25) shows verbal processes:

Jack	Said	'I'm sick'
Sayer	Process	Quoted
Quoting		

Mohammed	Said	he succeeded in
Sayer	Process	the exam
Reproting		Reported

Figure (25): Examples of verbal processes.

Chapter Two

Contrastive Grammar of Arabic

2.1 **Subject, Actor, Theme in Arabic :**

In Arabic, the subject in the unmarked nominal and verbal clauses may be a multifunctional item, i.e. the subject has more than one function at the same time. In nominal clauses, for example, the inchoative is the theme of the clause and it is the subject as well. Consider:

الطفل جميل   (The child (is) beautiful)

In , the child is the one with whom the message is concerned, and it is the subject by which the truth of the statement is vested in him. This can be illustrated in the following figure (1):

جميل	الطفل
Rheme	Theme subject

Figure (1): An inchoative of a nominal clauses functioning as Theme and Subject.

Adopting Hallidayian view (1994: 30), the theme and subject are equated

with psychological and grammatical subject. Thus (figure 1) can be:

جميل	الطفل
	psychological subject grammatical subject

Figure (2): An inchoative functioning as psychological and grammatical subject.

It should be noted here that the initial element, the inchoative functions as the Theme of the clause, i.e. what is being talked about. The enunciative, however, is considered the Rheme, what is being said about the Theme. Other examples are listed in figure 3):

صافية جميلة	السماء القصيدة	(The sky is clear) (The poem is beautiful)
Rheme	Theme	

الطفل	جميل
grammatical Theme	psychological Theme

Figure (3): Examples of nominal clauses with Theme-Rheme distinction.

As for the given and new information, the inchoative is given information, something known to the hearer, while the Rheme conveys the new information about the Theme (Aziz, 1997: 134).

So, in the unmarked pattern of nominal clauses, i.e. the order in inchoative-enunciative, the Theme is conflated with subject. However, in marked nominal clauses, the inchoative is no longer Theme. Instead, the fronted predicate has the thematic function. In other words, the order inchoative-enunciative is changed.

However, in the unmarked verbal clauses, the agent has more than one function at the same time, i.e. the agent is ascribed to different functions in the unmarked pattern which are subject and actor, e.g.

a. شرب الطفل الحليب (lit.) Drank the child milk

(The child drank the milk)

In (a), 'The child' is the subject of the clause in that the truth or falsehood of the statement is vested in him. Also, he is the actor who does the action of drinking. Thus, the two functions of subject and actor are conflated in 'the child'. But, الطفل 'the child' is not considered the theme of the clause because it is the verb in the unmarked verbal clause that functions as theme (Aziz, 1997: 134f):

الحليب	الطفل	شرب

	subject actor	Theme

Figure (4): Unmarked pattern of a verbal clause.

Strictly speaking, the subject and actor are equated with grammatical and logical subject respectively. The grammatical subject refers to the fact that there is person and number concord between the agent and the verb. This can be shown by the following rules (Wright, 1971: 37).

a) if the agent is singular feminine, it immediately follows the verb which is put in feminine:

جاءت ليلى –   (lit.) Came Layla

                             (Layla Came)

جاء محمد –   (lit.) Came Mohammed

                             (Mohammed Came)

b) if the agent is plural masculine the preceding verb is singular, e.g.

قال الرجال –   (lit.) Said the men

                             (The men said)

On the other hand, the logical subject refers to the one who does the action. Thus, figure (4) will be:

الحليب	الطفل	شرب
	- grammatical S. - logical S.	Theme

Figure (5): An agent functioning as grammatical and logical subject.

However, in marked clauses, the agent functions as subject, actor, Theme or grammatical, logical and psychological subject respectively. That is, these three functions of the agent can be combined or conflated in the marked thematic pattern of the clause:

الطفل شرب الحليب–   (The child drank milk)

الطفل 'the child', here, is the logical subject of the action, and it is the grammatical subject of the clause and the psychological subject who is the one with whom the message is concerned. This can be shown below:

الحليب	شرب	الطفل
		- grammatical S. (subject) - logical S. (actor) - psychological S. (Theme)

Figure (6): An agent functions as grammatical, logical and psychological subject.

It is worth noting that the subject-verb inversion or the deviation from the unmarked pattern VSO to SVO enables the speaker to select the subject as a thematic element which is given information.

In what follows, we are going to shed light on these functions in the clause.

- The theme (or psychological subject) functions in the structure of the clause as a message.
- The subject (or grammatical subject) in the structure of the clause as an exchange.
- The actor (or logical subject) in the structure of the clause as representation.

2.2 <u>Arabic Clause as a Message:</u>

2.2.1 <u>Unmarked and Marked Theme:</u>

Theme is a meaningful choice, so the speakers have the ability to choose between a marked and unmarked option. In Arabic, unmarked theme coincides with the first constituent of each mood structure. Thus, it is the subject in a declarative nominal clause, the verb in a declarative verbal clause, the polar interrogatives and the question words in interrogative clauses. In other words, the clause elements function as follows (Aziz, 1998: 122):

a) the NP in a nominal clause:

محمد مهندس-   (Mohammed (is) an engineer)

b) the verb in a verbal clause:

جاء الطالب-   (lit.) Came the student (The student came)

c) the particle أ or هل in polar questions:

هل أنت بخير؟-   (Are you allright?)

d) the question word in information questions:

من قال هذا؟-   (Who said this?)

e) the verbal element in directives:

أغلق الشباك-   (Close the window)

Following Halliday (1994: 61) in patterns (c) the Theme extends to the immediately following words, e.g.

<u>هل أنت-</u>   in   هل أنت بخير؟

Since Arabic has the ability to change the word order, and especially by fronting the element to the initial position of the clause, there is a wide range of marked thematic patterns. They are as follow:

a) the subject in verbal clauses:

محمد أكرم خالداً (Mohammed honored Khalid)

b) the object in a statement:

الفستان اشتريته   (The dress I bought)

c) a nominal element functioning as subject, object or adverbial in a question:

أخوك هل حضر الحفلة (s.)   (Your brother, did he attend the party?)

الكتاب هل اشتريته؟   (o.)   (The book, did you buy it?)

(Aziz, 1997: 194)

d) the subject in imperative clauses:

يا أنت أفتح الباب   (You, open the door)

Turning back to subject, we can say that the unmarked theme in nominal declarative clauses is the inchoative and it is the agent which is the marked theme in verbal ones. Let us consider the following figures:

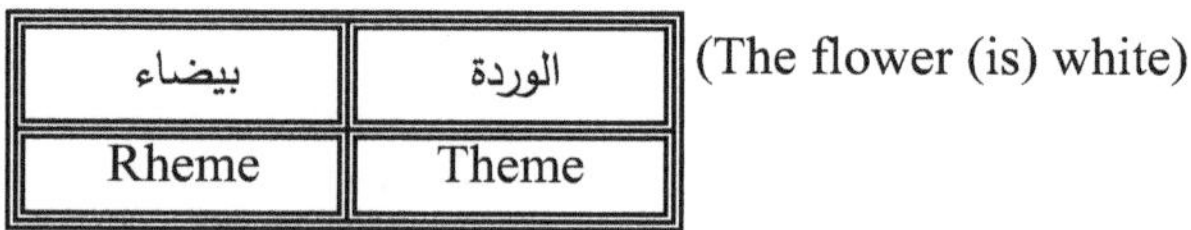

(The flower (is) white)

Figure (7): Theme in the unmarked nominal clause.

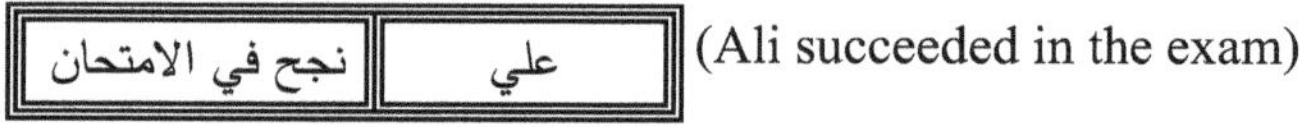

(Ali succeeded in the exam)

50

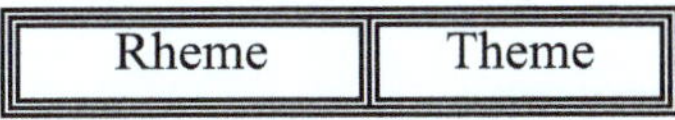

Figure (8): Theme in the marked verbal clause.

It should be noted here that in the nominal clauses, the inchoative is no longer thematized in the marked pattern (see 4.1.1.1), e.g.

(White is the flower)

Figure (9): Theme in the marked nominal clause.

To summarize, markedness is associated with the unusual word order. That is, Theme-Rheme distinction in Arabic nominal clauses is realized by the usual sequence of elements in the clause inchoative-enunciative المبتدأ–الخبر. So, the Theme is the first element in the sequence which is usually given information. In the marked pattern, however, there is a change of the word order, i.e. the sequence inchoative-enunciative is changed into enunciative-inchoative. The same can be said about verbal clauses. The normal word order is the verb-agent-complement. However, the verb is considered the Theme in the unmarked patterns, while in the marked pattern the Theme is no longer the verb but the agent. Consequently, the word sequence becomes agent-verb-complement.

Another point to be made here is that the subject (or the inchoative) in the unmarked nominal clause is usually given information, while the predicate (or the enunciative) is new information. In other words, the Theme in the unmarked patterns of nominal clauses is given while the Rheme is new. Consider :

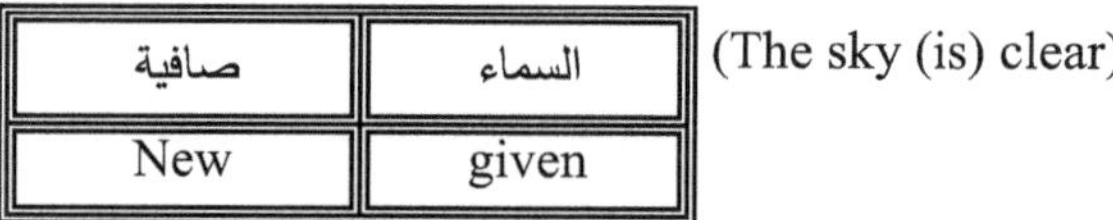

Figure (10): Information distinction in unmarked nominal clause.

The marked Theme, however, in nominal clauses may be given information, whereas the inchoative becomes new. Hence, the above figure would be as follows:

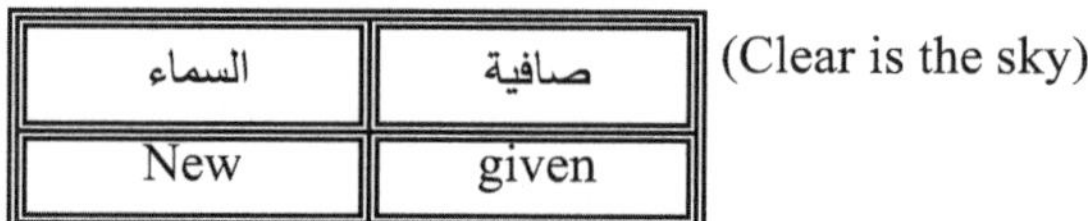

Figure (11): Information distinction in marked nominal clause.

Furthermore, what is said about nominal clauses can be said about verbal ones. That is, in the unmarked pattern, the verb (or the predicate) is usually given, whereas the subject (or the agent) is new.

a. 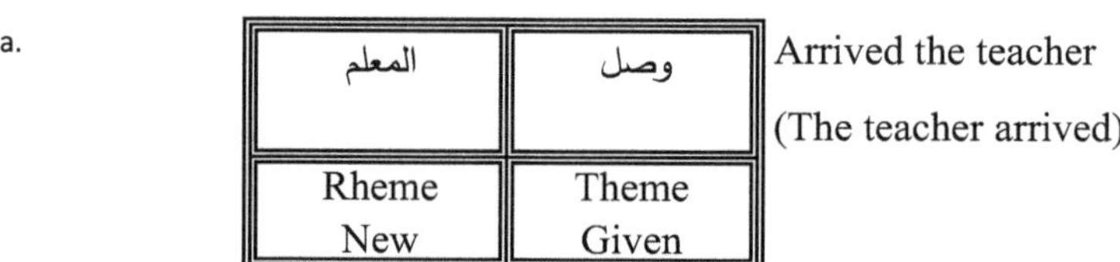

Figure (12): Information distinction in the unmarked verbal clause.

As we have already mentioned, Theme is the starting point of the speaker. So, it carries given information. On the other hand, Rheme carries new information by which the message reaches its end. In (a) above, with the neutral reading on the final element of the clause, the verb is considered the Theme which is given information, while Rheme is the agent which is new. However, in the marked pattern, i.e. وصل المعلم (The teacher arrived), the Theme is the agent which is given, while the verb is new. This is due to the fact that as a thematic structure, Theme has a less burden of information, coming at the beginning of the sentence. Rheme, has more information which is usually placed at the end of the sentence (Aziz, 1997: 133). Hence, the given information is related to Theme, while new to Rheme as illustrated below:

b.
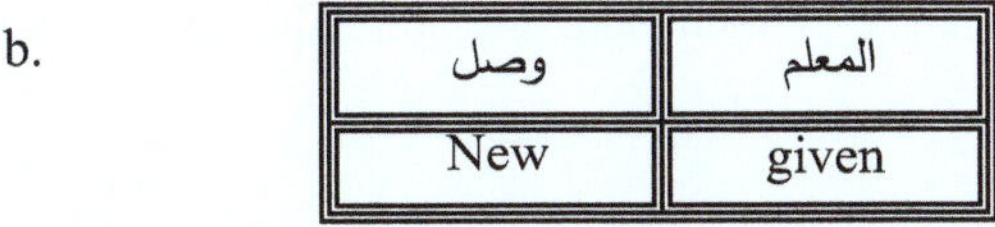

Figure (13): Information distinction in the marked verbal clause.

Strictly speaking, (a) can be an answer to (What did the teacher do?) وصل المعلم . However, (b) is a reply to (Who arrived?)المعلم وصل. Thus, the Theme usually comes at the beginning of the sentence with the given information. But, Rheme has the new information which comes at the end of the sentence (ibid.: 135).

As for the interrogative clauses in Arabic, they are of two main types: polarity questions and information questions. Polarity questions require yes or no answers. However, wh-questions need information. No word order is utilized to indicate the types of the interrogative

53

clause because this is indicated by using appropriate particles or question words (Aziz, 1989: 253).

Polarity questions are introduced by means of two particles هل and أ.

هل قمت بواجبك؟	(Have you done your homework?)
أ أنت بخير؟	(Are you fine?)

Halliday (1994: 46) argues that interrogatives express questions, the natural Theme of a question is 'I want to be told ',the answer is either a piece of information or an indication of polarity. So, in Arabic, the realization of this interrogative mood is expressed by the particles أ or هل in polarity questions, and the questions words in content questions. Following Halliday (ibid.: 46; Aziz, 1997: 61), in yes/no interrogatives, there is a two-part Theme. It consists of the particle or the interrogative element and the immediately following words. Examples are in figure (14):

بواجباتك	قمت	هل
بخير	أنت	أ
Rheme	Theme 2	Theme 1

Figure (14): A Theme in Arabic yes/no questions.

In most cases of such interrogatives, the particle has the interpersonal Theme and the topical Theme is the ideational element which is immediately following the interrogative word. Thus, examples in figure (15) will be as follows:

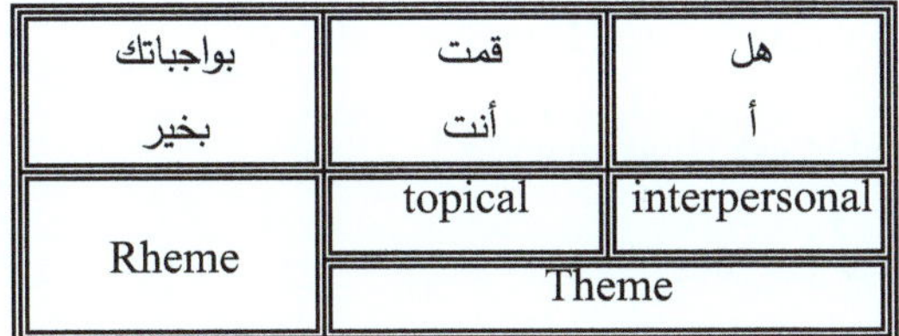

بواجباتك بخير	قمت أنت	هل أ
	topical	interpersonal
Rheme	Theme	

Figure (15): Components of thematic structure of Arabic yes/no questions.

However, content interrogatives ask about one of the elements of the clause. They begin by one of the following question words:

(1) من (who) which is used to ask about persons

من جاء؟ (Who came?)

(2) ما (what) which is used to ask about things

ما فعلتَ؟ (What did you do?)

(3) ماذا (what) which is used for things

ماذا وجدت؟ (What did you find?)

(4) أي (which) which is used with definite or indefinite noun

أي كتاب تفضل؟ (Which book do you prefer?)

(5) أين (where) which is used to ask about place.

أين ذهبت؟ (Where did you go?)

(6) متى (when). It is used to ask about time

متى زرت ليلى؟ (When did you visit Layla?)

(7) كم (how many, how much)

كم بحثاً كتبت؟ (How many papers have you written?)

(8) كيف (how) which is used to ask about manner

كيف حالك؟ (How are you?)

(9) لماذا (why) to ask about reasons

لماذا فشلت في الامتحان؟ (Why did you fail?)

In such interrogative clauses, the Theme is constituted by the content element. Examples can be represented as follows:

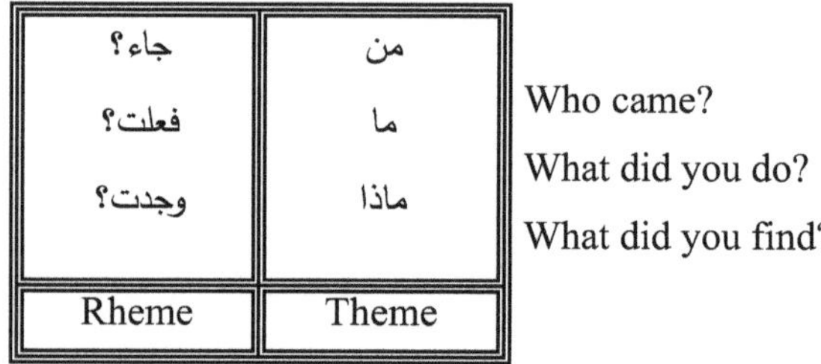

Who came?
What did you do?
What did you find?

Figure (16): Theme and Rheme in content interrogatives.

It should be clarified, here, that in Arabic, the general tendency for the speaker is to choose the unmarked Theme pattern. However, the marked Theme is introduced by placing elements other than the question words in front:

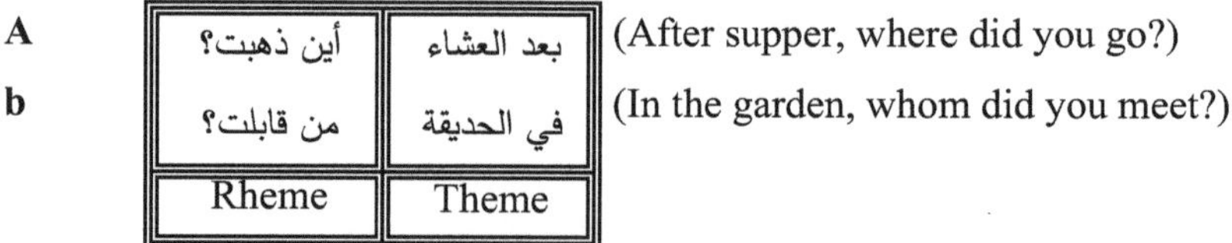

(After supper, where did you go?)

(In the garden, whom did you meet?)

Figure (17): Examples of Arabic marked Theme.

In (a), the adverbial group بعد العشاء (after supper) is fronted, i.e. the usual sequence of (a) is أين ذهبت بعد العشاء؟ (Where did you go after supper?) QVSA, but in (b), the adverbial group comes in front of the question word, the verb and the implicit subject or agent أنت . Thus, the marked Theme is realized by بعد العشاء (after supper).

To sum up, the unmarked Theme is the inchoative in the nominal clause, the verb in the verbal clause, the question words in interrogative clauses. So, if elements other than the above-mentioned ones function as Themes, they are, then, marked.

2.2.2 Simple and Multiple Themes:

Another distinction drawn by Halliday (1985: 41) is between simple and multiple Theme. In Arabic a simple Theme is one which is realized by a single element which is ideational in meaning. In other words, an element which represents a process, a participant in a process or a circumstance associated with that process (ibid.: 52). So, the simple Theme could either be the inchoative in the nominal clause or the verb in the verbal clause. Also, that element could be realized by an adverbial group or prepositional phrase as in:

a.
b.

Rheme	Theme
رأيت علياً	في الدار
جاء محمد	ضاحكاً

(At home, I saw Ali)

(Smilingly, Mohammed came)

Figure (18): Simple Themes in Arabic.

The Theme may have more than one group, but it is still said to be simple, because the groups formed a single constituent in the structure of the clause (ibid.: 40). In Arabic, the nominal declarative clause has more than one inchoative (Al-Makhzumi, 1966: 152). Such groups are called group complex functioning as Theme:

a.

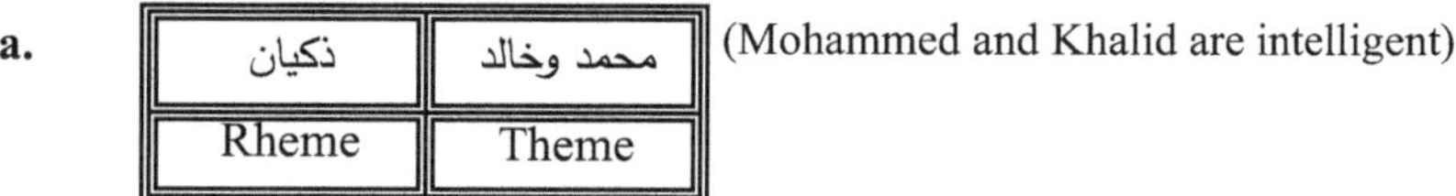

Rheme	Theme
ذكيان	محمد وخالد

(Mohammed and Khalid are intelligent)

Figure (19): A group complex as Theme.

In (a), the group complex محمد وخالد (Mohammed and Khalid) are two nominal groups joined by the coordinator (واو), forming a nominal group complex. Similarly, two prepositional phrases make up a prepositional phrase complex which is considered one simple Theme. An example of this would be:

من الشمال إلى الجنوب العراق وطن واحد

(From north to south, Iraq is a one country)

Also, there is, in Arabic, an equative structure of the identifier-identified which is a type of equational construction equivalent to the Thematic Equation in which the Theme and Rheme are put in the form of equation. In other words, all the elements of the clause are put into two constituents which are linked by a relationship of identity. One constituent specifies the Theme, while the other equates Theme with Rheme. Let us consider the following example:

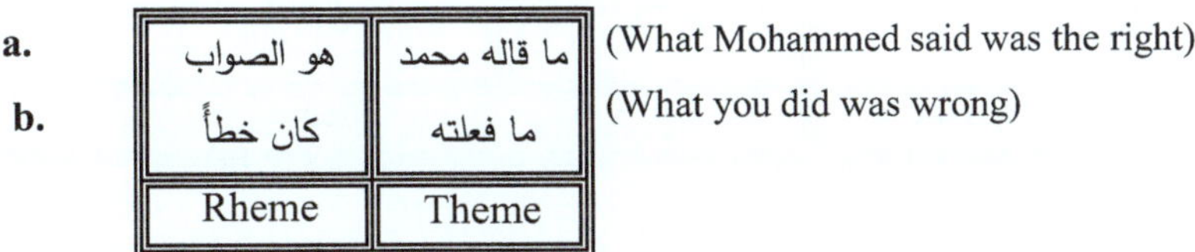

Figure (20): Examples of equatives in Arabic.

Halliday (1994: 54) defines the multiple Theme as one in which the topical Theme is preceded by interpersonal and textual Themes. That is, the multiple Theme has three components: textual Theme, interpersonal Theme and ideational (or topical) Theme. In Arabic, it was found that a Theme may have three types of meaning: the ideational, interpersonal and textual as in the following example (Abdullah, 1991: 54):

ولكن أ أنت اشتراكي مخلص

(But are you a committed socialist?)

(Mahfuz, 1974: 155)

As shown above, the Theme is of three components: الهمزة أ , ولكن , and أنت The first component which is the conjunction 'ولكن' which indicates the relationship of the clause with the preceding one in the text. This component is called the textual Theme. The second element is the interrogative particle أ which represents the interpersonal component. The last element is the topical Theme which is an ideational element which represents a process, a participant in a process or a circumstance. The topical Theme, then, is preceded by the interpersonal and textual Themes. Consider the following figure :

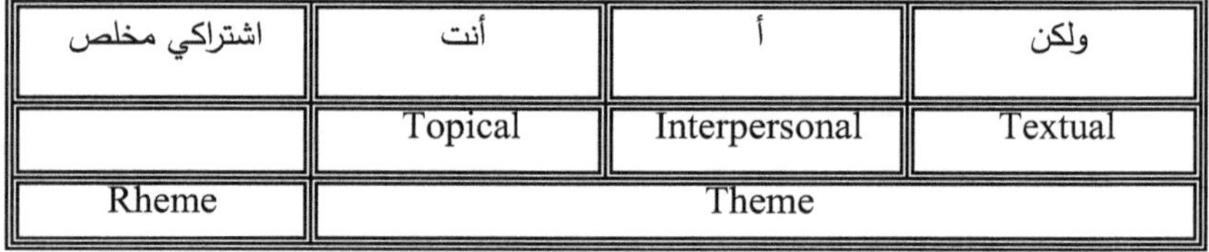

اشتراكي مخلص	أنت	أ	ولكن
	Topical	Interpersonal	Textual
Rheme	Theme		

Figure (21): An example of multiple Theme in Arabic.

We can say that the topical Theme is realized by the subject (or the inchoative in the nominal clause) preceded by the interpersonal and textual Theme.

It should be mentioned, here, that in Arabic, the interpersonal Theme will be:

a) The interrogative particles أ and هل in polar interrogatives, e.g.

هل عزمت على الرحيل؟ (Are you leaving?)

(Mahfuz, 1974: 51)

b) Question words in content interrogatives, e.g.

أين ذهبت؟   (Where did you go?)

c) Vocative

صفا أسرعي   (Safa ... hurry up!)

d) A modal Theme which expresses modality, e.g. لعل (perhaps), the

adverbs ربما (may be), لابد (certainly), من المحتمل (probably).

However, the textual Theme in Arabic is realized by one or more items which relate the clause to the preceding one. The textual Theme may be a combination of the following:

a) Continuatives such as نعم (yes), حسناً (well), الآن (now). Such words mark that a new move is beginning.

b) Conjunctions are of two types: coordinators and subordinators. The coordinators و (and), the coordinator ف , ثُم (then), and لكنْ (but) (Aziz, 1989: 212-213), e.g.

علي مدرس و زوجته طبيبة   (Ali is a teacher and his wife is a doctor)

درس فنجح في الامتحان   (He studied so he succeeded in the exam)

It should be noted that the meaning of the coordinator و is that of the English (and). As for ف , the basic meaning is sequence, i.e. the action of the second clause immediately follows the first one.

The subordinators, however, are the linking particles أن (إنّ) (that), those in adverbial clauses of place حيثما (wherever), time لمّا (when), cause لأن (because), condition إذا، إن، لو، لولا if and the subordinators كأن (as if), and بينما (while) (ibid.: 22ff). Examples are:

إن تدرس تنجح   (If you study, you will succeed)

جلس حيثما جلس أخوه من قبل   (He sat wherever his brother had sat before)

c) Relative Pronouns: They are of two types. The first type introduces a clause postmodifying a noun head, while the second is used pronominally. The first type includes الذي (masculine) with its dual subjective اللذان and objective and genitive اللذين and the plural الذين and the feminine التي، اللتان، اللتين، اللواتي، اللاتي , e.g.

الرجل الذي قابلته   (The man that I met ...)

The relative pronoun (الذي) is the textual Theme.

d) Conjunctive adjuncts such as أيْ (that is), على أية حال (however), أيضاً (also), لهذا السبب (therefore), أخيراً (finally), رغم ذلك (despite that), etc.

على أية حال فأنت شاب تتمناك أية فتاة

(At any rate, you are a young man fancied by all girls)

(Mahfuz, 1974: 67)

المشهدواخيراً، انتهى(Finally, the scene came to an end)

What we have to say, here, about, Arabic multiple Theme is that the topical Theme comes last and it is preceded by the interpersonal Theme as illustrated in the following figures:

بصحة جيدة؟	أنت	هل	و	(And are you in a good health?)
		interrogative particle	Coordinator	
	topical	interpersonal	Textual	
Rheme	Theme			

حزين؟	أنت	لماذا	حسنٌ	(Well, why are you sad?)
		content interrogative	Continuative	
Rheme	topical	interpersonal	Textual	
	Theme			

Figure (22): Examples of multiple Theme in Arabic.

It should be stressed, here, that Arabic multiple Theme has no explicit topical Theme. That is, the topical (or ideational Theme) is the implied third person, e.g.

ولماذا فشل في الامتحان؟

(And why he failed in the exam)

Here, the components of multiple Theme are only the textual Theme and the interpersonal Theme. The analysis of this clause is shown below:

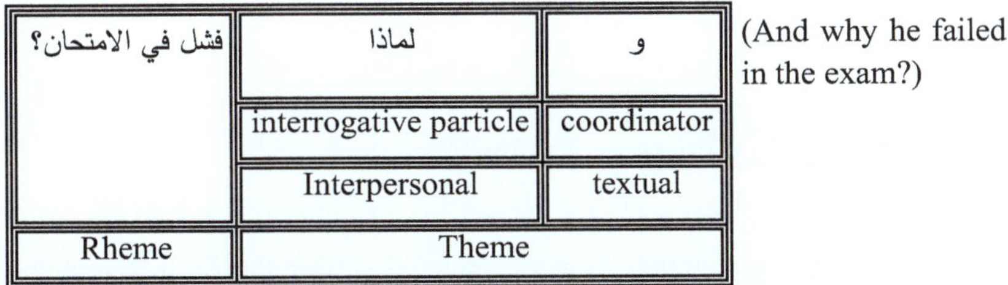

<table>
<tr><td rowspan="3">فشل في الامتحان؟</td><td colspan="2">لماذا</td><td>و</td><td rowspan="3">(And why he failed in the exam?)</td></tr>
<tr><td>interrogative particle</td><td>coordinator</td></tr>
<tr><td>Interpersonal</td><td>textual</td></tr>
<tr><td>Rheme</td><td colspan="3">Theme</td><td></td></tr>
</table>

Figure (23): An example of multiple theme with implicit topical Theme

As illustrated above, the particle 'لم' is utilized to negate the declarative verbal clause (يقرأ علي الكتب). So, it is functionally considered a finite element. Other examples are given below:

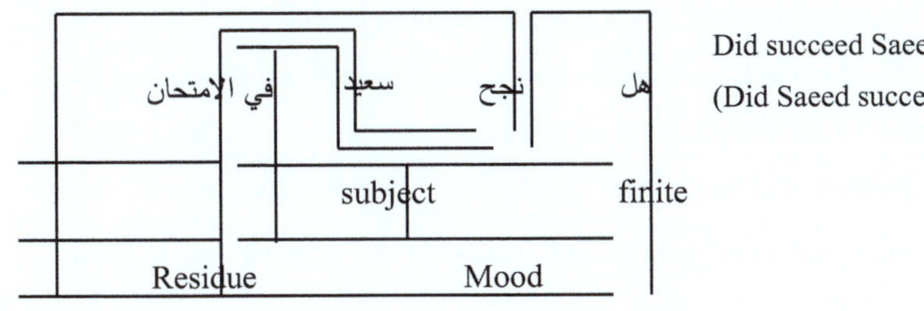

Did succeed Saeed in the exam
(Did Saeed succeed in the exam?)

Figure (24): Structure of Arabic interrogative clause.

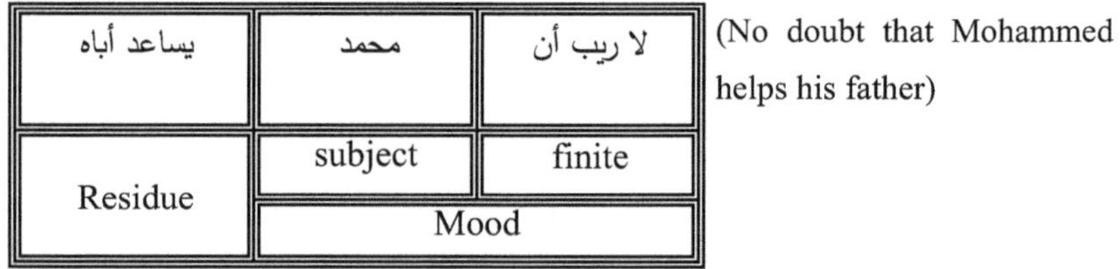

يساعد أباه	محمد	لا ريب أن	(No doubt that Mohammed helps his father)
	subject	finite	
Residue	Mood		

Figure (25): Structure of Arabic declarative clause conveying certainty.

2.3 <u>Arabic Clause as Exchange:</u>

In the last sections, we set out an interpretation of the Arabic clause in its function as a message, describing it as a two-element structure with Theme-Rheme. In what follows, we shall discuss another function of the Arabic clause, viz. its meaning as an exchange. The grammatical system here is mood.

Halliday (1994: 68) argues that the clause is organized as an interactive event involving the speaker and the hearer. In the act of speaking, the speaker adopts a certain speech role, and he assigns to the listener a complementary role. That is, the speaker is giving something to the hearer (a piece of information) or he is demanding something for him. That is why Halliday claims that the basic types of speech roles are just two: giving and demanding (ibid.).

The system of the clause as an exchange is Mood which carries the burden of the clause as an interactive event between different roles of the speaker and the hearer. In Arabic, there are five moods: the indicative (الرفع), the subjunctive (النصب), the jussive (الجزم), the imperative (الأمر) and the emphatic التوكيد (Wright, 1971: 24; Aziz, 1989: 79).

The indicative mood is the unmarked in Arabic. It is used with the imperfect with ُ (dhamma) at its end and the perfect َ (alfatha), e.g.

يكتبُ محمد الرسالةَ   Writes Mohammed the letter

                              (Mohammed writes the letter)

The subjunctive mood is used after certain particles such as لن which governs the imperfect verb in the subjunctive. In what follows, the particles which govern the verb in the subjunctive mood are listed:

i)   لن negation for the future

لن أحضر الاجتماع   (lit.) Not attend the meeting

                              (I won't attend the meeting)

ii)   أنْ it is used in complementary of certain verbs, e.g.

أود أنْ أتكلمَ معك   (I wish I could talk to you)

iii)   كي، لكي (so that)

درستُ كي انجحَ   (I studied to succeed)

iv)   حتى (till, until)

قرأ حتى ينجحَ   (He studied to succeed)

v)   فـ which is known فاء السببية (فاء for purposes) which express causes

vi)   أو (until, unless), e.g.

لاستسهلن الصعب أو أدرك المنى
(I'll consider all difficult things easy until I attain my aim)

(Aziz, 1989:80)

<u>The jussive mood</u> is used with the imperfect verb only. It is used after the jussive particles such as لم and لما which indicate negation in the past, e.g.

لم أرهْ في المكتبة   (I didn't see him in the library)

لما يكتبْ الواجب لحد الآن   (He has not written the homework yet)

Also, the jussive mood is used in clauses with the imperative implication after the particle لِ (let) called (Lam of command) and which is used in 3rd person and 1st person plural (Wright, 1971: 35). For example,

لنلعب في الحديقة   (Let's play in the garden)

This is also a common use in prohibitions after the particle لا which is called (the la of prohibition) in connection with which it expresses a prohibition or a wish that something may not be achieved:

لا تفعل هذا ثانية   (Don't do this again)

In addition, the jussive mood is utilized in conditional clauses which depend on إنَ or any particle with the sense of إنْ. It stands in the superordinate and the subordinate clauses of sentences, e.g.

إن تقتربْ أكثر تشعلْ إصبعك

(If you come closer your finger will be burnt).

The other particles which are considered conditional are the indefinite pronouns مَن (whoever), مهما (whatever) and the adverbials حيثما, أينما (wherever) and كيفما (however):

من يعملْ خيراً يُجزَ به   (He who does good, shall be rewarded)

حيثما تذهبْ أذهب   (Wherever you go I'll go)

The <u>imperative mood</u> is used with the second person to give orders and commands. It is derived from the jussive form by omitting the prefix of the imperfect ـِ and replacing it by أ if the second radical has الضمة (dhamma) or الكسرة (kasra) or الفتحة (fatha). This is done to avoid a consonant cluster which is not preferable in Arabic. However, if there is no a consonant cluster in a word, the prefix أ is not used (Aziz, 1989: 82):

نظف الغرفة   (Clean the room)

The <u>energetic mood</u> is formed from the jussive by adding نّ or نْ with the particle لـ , نوني التوكيد

لتكتبنّ الواجب   (You are to write the homework)

Also, the energetic mood may be used in the following:

a) in prohibitions, commands, wishes and questions (Wright, 1971: 42), e.g.

لا تكسرنَّ الشبك   (Do not break the window)

b) in correlative conditional sentences when the particle لـ is prefixed to the conditional ئن as well as to the verb in the superordinate clause:

لئنْ قلت هذا لتندمْ   (If you say this you will regret)

c) after حيثما and إما and the indefinite particle ما:

فأمـا ترين أحد فأخبره   (If you should see anyone, you'll tell him)

بجهدٍ ما تبلغنَّ

(With some painstaking you'll certainly accomplish it)

(ibid.: 43)

What is more significant, however, is that the mood system, in Arabic, is expressed only in the verbal clauses. Thus, the nominal clauses will not be considered in our analysis.

On the other hand, we have remarked that mood is of two components subject and the finite (Halliday, 1994: 74). The finiteness, then, is expressed by means of tense, modality or polarity features. Following Halliday (1994), the subject is the responsible element for doing the action. As for the finite element, it is expressed by three ways: tense, modality and polarity. In Arabic, however, there is no grammatical classification between auxiliary and lexical (Aziz, 1989: 29). That is, there are two main tenses in Arabic: present with the imperfect and past with the perfect. To make negative and interrogative clauses, some particles such as لا، لم and لن are used.

More specifically, the particles لا، لم and لن are used to negate the declarative clauses:

a.لا أعرف السبب	(I don't know the reason)
b.لن أكتب البحث	(I won't write the paper)
c.لم اقل هذا	(I didn't say this)

Similarly, Arabic questions are realized by means of certain particles as هل and أ. There is no change in the word order, e.g.

a.هل رأيت محمداً؟	(Did you see Mohammed?)
b.أ أنت جاد؟	(Are you serious?)

So, the declarative clause of (299a) is (رأيت محمد) (I saw Mohammed). That is, there is no change of the word order of declarative clauses to make interrogative clauses in which the negative particle هل is used only, changing a declarative clauses into an interrogative one.

The same can be said about modality. In Arabic, there are no modal verbs which form a group realizing modality and modulation (Aziz, 1989: 84). In fact, different lexical words or expressions are utilized to express the basic meanings of each. These meanings will be dealt with below.

The meanings of modality are certainty, possibility and probability. Certainty is expressed by either verbs such as يجب and ينبغي or expressions like يجب أن يكون, لابد أن, e.g.

لابد أن تأتي   (You must come)

Possibility, however, is also expressed by either verbs such as يمكن , يحتمل or the particle قد:

يمكن ان تحل المسألة(You may solve the question)

As for probability, it can be conveyed by verbs like يُظن، يرجح. Also, the prepositional phrases as من المرجح، من الأرجح and the constructions أغلب الظن are used. Consider these examples:

من المرجح أن تسافر ليلى غدام   (It is probably that Layla will travel tomorrow)

However, the major meanings of modulation are as follows:

- Ability: The verbs used for carrying ability are يقدر، يتمكن، يستطيع , etc.

- Willingness: The verbs used are يريد، يبغي , e.g.

- ذا أردت أن تأتي معنا   (If you want to come with us)

- Permission: It is used by means of imperative mood (Aziz, 1989: 85)

أدخل الآن   (Come in now)

Thus, from a functional point of view, the finite element of the Arabic verbal clause includes these particles and expressions as shown in the following figure:

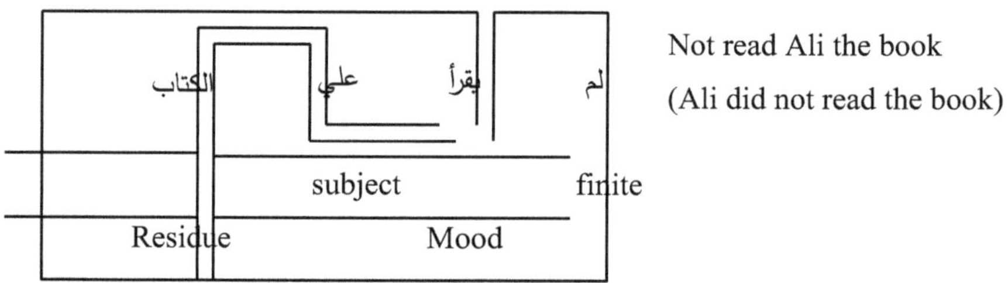

Figure (26): A structure of Arabic unmarked negative declarative clause.

This is clearly expressed in the marked pattern:

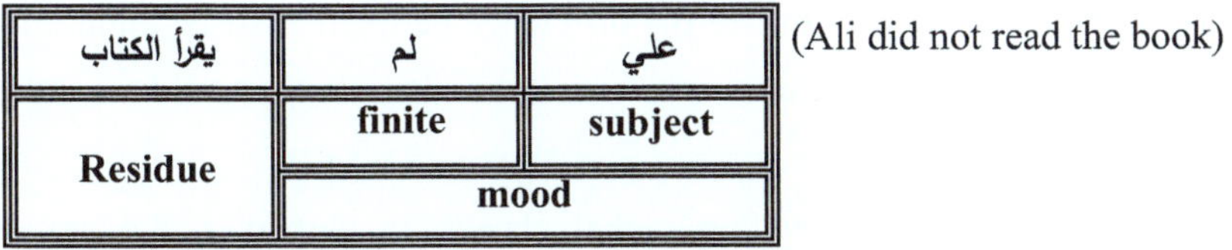

(Ali did not read the book)

Figure (27): Structure of marked negative clause.

As illustrated above, the particle 'لم' is utilized to negate the declarative verbal clause (يقرأ علي الكتب). So, it is functionally considered a finite element. Other examples are given below:

2.4 <u>Arabic Clause as Representation:</u>

In the preceding section, we dealt with the meaning of the Arabic clause as an exchange or its interpersonal function. In this section, however, we shall discuss the clause in its experiential function, i.e. its use as a means of representing patterns of experience. Halliday (1994: 106) argues that the most powerful impression of experience is that it consists of 'goings-on', happening, doing, sensing, meaning. Consequently, the clause is a mode of reflection of the events. This is achieved by the grammatical system of Transitivity which construes the experience world into a set of process types. Here, we should highlight the difference between inner and outer experience, i.e. between what we experience inside and outside ourselves. In other

71

words, we have to utilize the difference between what is going on in the world of imagination and what is out there in the world around us (ibid.).

In Arabic, and in verbal clauses in particular, the process consists of three components: The process, participants in the process and the circumstances through which the process is achieved, e.g.

a. جاء محمد مسرعاً   (Came Mohammed in a hurry)

(Mohammed came in a hurry)

In (a), جاء (came) is a process, محمد (Mohammed) is a participant in the process, and مسرعاً (in a hurry) is the circumstance related to the process.

Generally speaking, the process is realized by a verb or a verbal group, the participant is realized by a nominal group; and the circumstance by an adverbial group as in the above example or a prepositional phrase as in the following example:

(b) سافر ياسين إلى بغداد   (lit.) Travelled Yassin to Baghdad

(Yassin travelled to Baghdad)

إلى بغداد	ياسين	سافر
Circumstance	participant	process
prepositional phrase	nominal group	a verbal group

Figure (28): Clause as process, participant and circumstance.

In what follows, we shall be concern with the process types and the participants in each.

2.4.1 Process Types:

2.4.1.1 Material Processes:

Material processes express actions or activities carried out by a participant called Agent. What we mean by an agent or a 'doer' is any entity that is able to bring about some change in the location or properties of itself or others (Dowing and Locke, 2002: 114). More importantly, if we examine these processes, we find that the subject is termed the Actor. In verbal clauses with intransitive verbs, there is one Actor or agent with no goal. However, this is not the case with clauses of transitive verbs in which the second participant is called the Goal

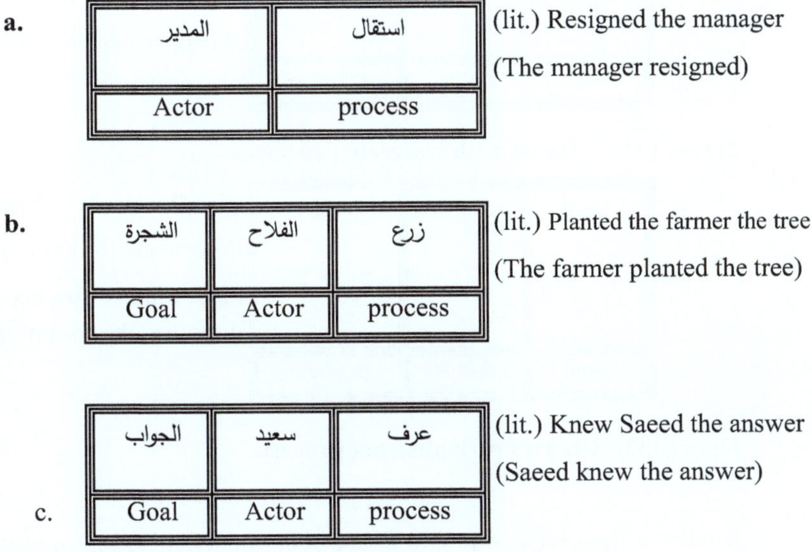

Figure (29): Examples of material processes in Arabic.

Taking these three examples into account, we can recognize that the material processes, in Arabic, are not only concrete but they may be abstract doings and happenings. In (a) we can recognize the verb 'استقال' 'resign' which is abstract, whereas in (b) and (c), there are concrete and physical events. Consider also:

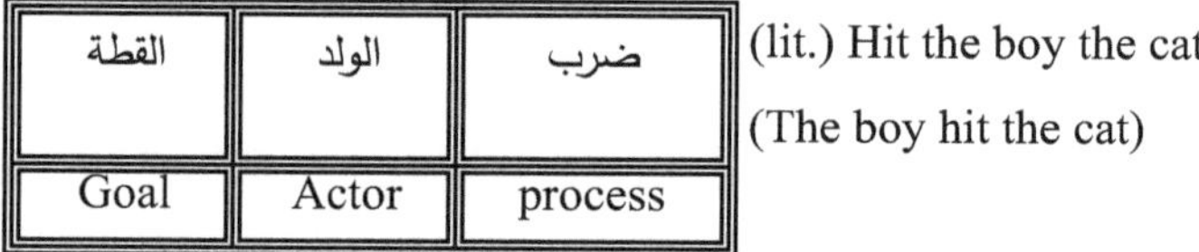

Figure (30): An example of concrete event in Arabic.

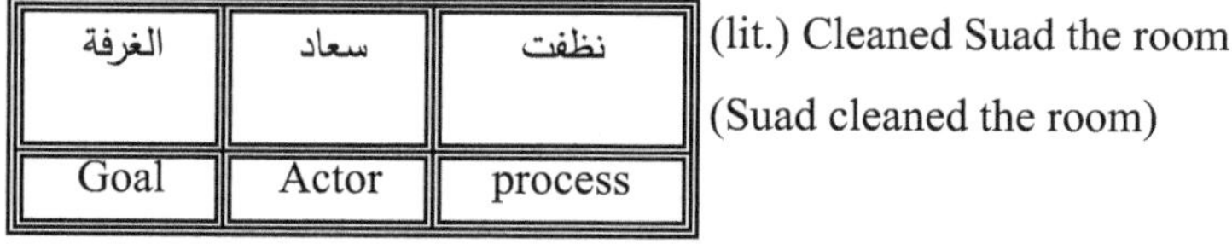

Figure (31): Clauses with concrete processes.

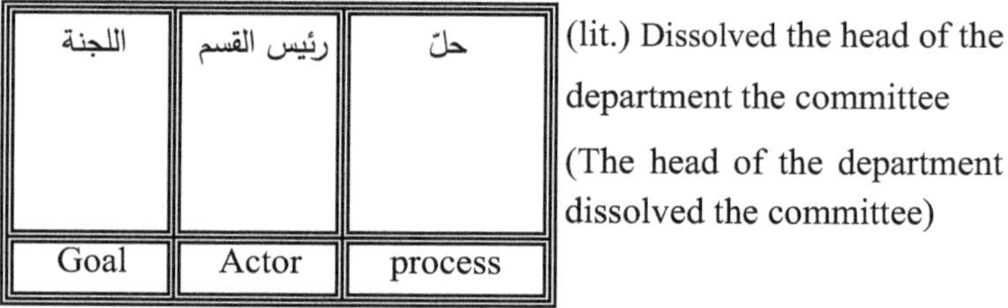

Figure (32): Clauses with abstract process.

It follows from what was said above about material processes is that the subject is called Actor.

2.4.1.2 <u>Mental Processes:</u>

In Arabic, we can hardly explain clauses by saying that they are doings or happenings. Thus, we shall recognize that there are other clauses in which the Actor-Goal trail does not work. It seems therefore necessary to find another functional interpretation of clauses which are termed Mental Process (Halliday, 1994: 112). In such clauses, the subject (or agent) is no longer an 'Actor'. Instead, it is called a <u>Sensor</u>. What is happening, here, is the subject in mental processes is the human who thinks, feels and he is conscious. That is, one distinction between material and mental clauses is that in the material clauses, the participant (subjects) may or may not be a human, e.g.

شربت القطة الحليب   (lit.) Drank the cat the milk

(The cat drank the milk)

This is, however, not the case with mental processes in which the Senser should be human.

On the other hand, the rest of the clause (apart from Sensor) is called phenomenon which is something that is sensed or felt as in figure (33):

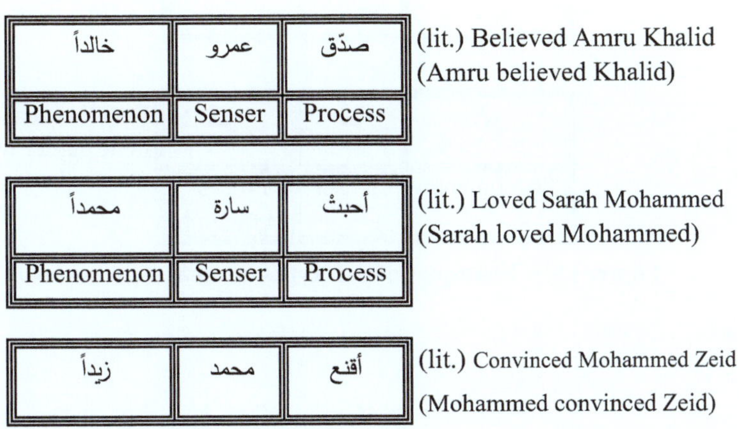

خالداً	عمرو	صدّق	(lit.) Believed Amru Khalid
Phenomenon	Senser	Process	(Amru believed Khalid)

محمداً	سارة	أحبّ	(lit.) Loved Sarah Mohammed
Phenomenon	Senser	Process	(Sarah loved Mohammed)

زيداً	محمد	أقنع	(lit.) Convinced Mohammed Zeid
			(Mohammed convinced Zeid)

Phenomenon	Senser	Process

Figure (33): Examples of mental processes.

Following Halliday (ibid.: 118), in Arabic, the sub-types, of mental process will be labelled: verbs of perception, such as سمع، رأى, verbs of affection أحب، أخاف and verbs of cognition, e.g. فهم، عرف . Let us consider the following examples below:

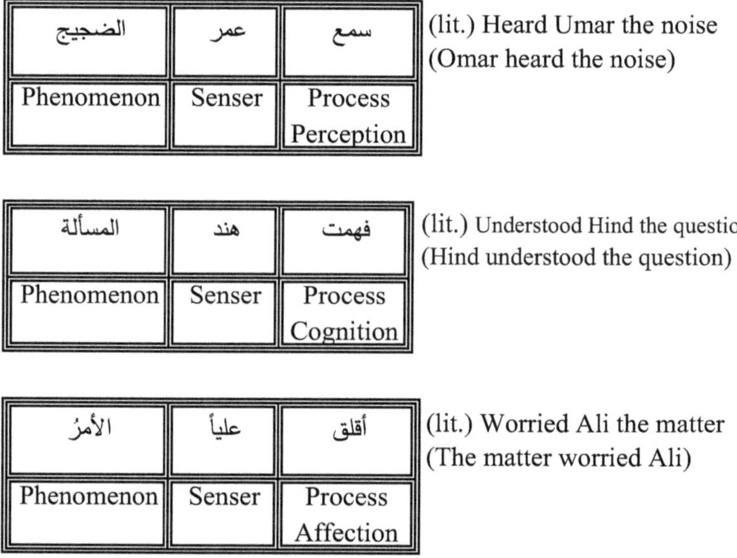

الضجيج	عمر	سمع	(lit.) Heard Umar the noise (Omar heard the noise)
Phenomenon	Senser	Process Perception	

المسألة	هند	فهمت	(lit.) Understood Hind the question (Hind understood the question)
Phenomenon	Senser	Process Cognition	

الأمرُ	علياً	أقلق	(lit.) Worried Ali the matter (The matter worried Ali)
Phenomenon	Senser	Process Affection	

Figure (34): Examples of sub-types of mental processes in Arabic.

It is useful to note that there are mental cognition processes as ،حسب

ظن (thought) which are ditransitive (Sibawayh, 1966: 36; Al-Makhzumi, 1966: 100). Examples are in the figure below:

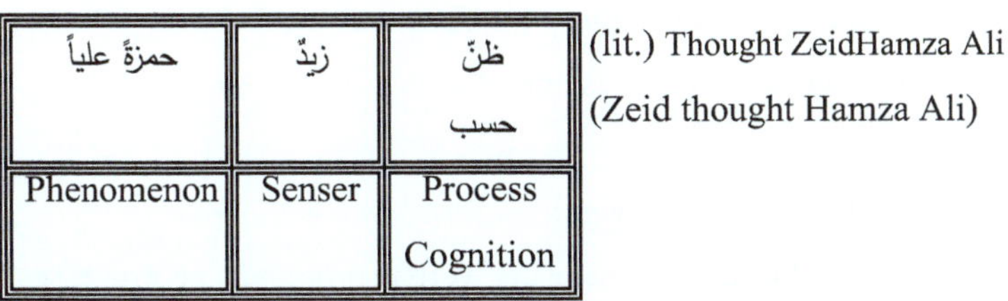

Figure (35): An example of the cognition process in Arabic.

In moving into the structure of these clauses, we find that Arab grammarians believe that the verbs حسب، ظن (thought) take two objects. Thus, in (320), حمزة is مفعول به أول (first object), and علياً is مفعول به ثاني (second object). However, Aziz (1989: 198), with whom we agree, believes that such structure is of SVOC, i.e. حمزة is مفعول به, while علياً is تكملة المفعول به.

2.4.1.3 Behavioural Process:

Following Halliday (1998: 139), in Arabic, there are processes of behaviour in which the grammatical function of the subject is labelled (Behaver) who is typically human. Let us consider the following:

a.

77

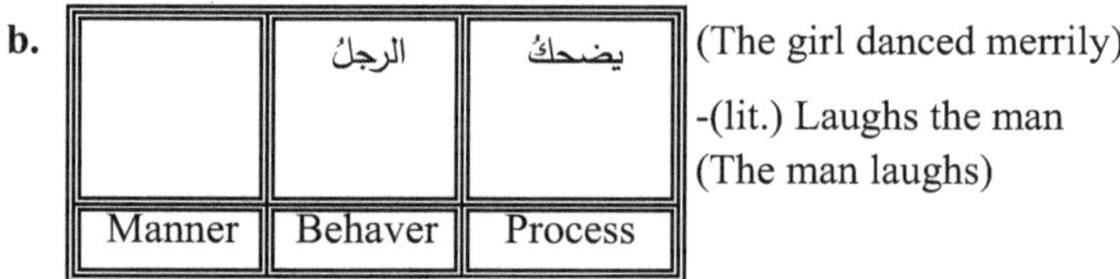

	الرجلُ	يضحكُ
Manner	Behaver	Process

(The girl danced merrily)

-(lit.) Laughs the man

(The man laughs)

Figure (36): Examples of behavioural processes.

In the above examples, we find that the behaver is a human being, whereas the process is one of doing.

2.4.1.4 <u>Verbal Process:</u>

In Arabic, there are verbal processes or processes of saying. The participant who is saying is labelled 'Sayer" and he is typically a conscious being. The indirect speech, in Arabic, has no change in the tense of verbs, but there will be changes in the pronouns and adverbs (Aziz, 1989: 277), e.g.

a. قال: انني على عجلة من أمري

(He said 'I am in a hurry) (Direct Speech)

b. قال إنه على عجلة من أمره

(He said that he was in a hurry)

From a functional viewpoint, however, the object of the verb 'say' functions as the subordinate clause in the clause complex. Let us consider the following figure:

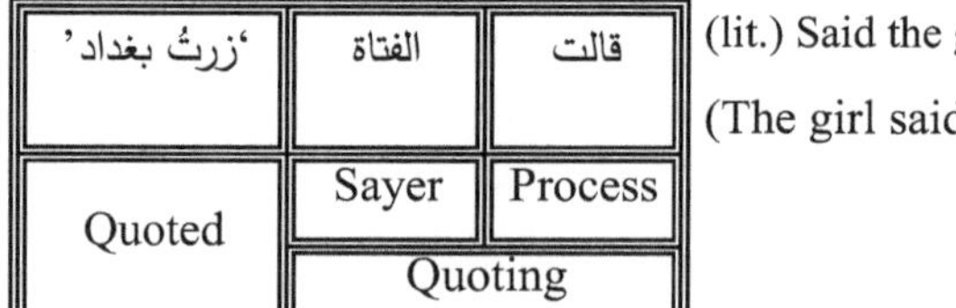

'زرتُ بغداد'	الفتاة	قالت
Quoted	Sayer	Process
	Quoting	

(lit.) Said the girl 'I visited Baghdad'

(The girl said 'I visited Baghdad')

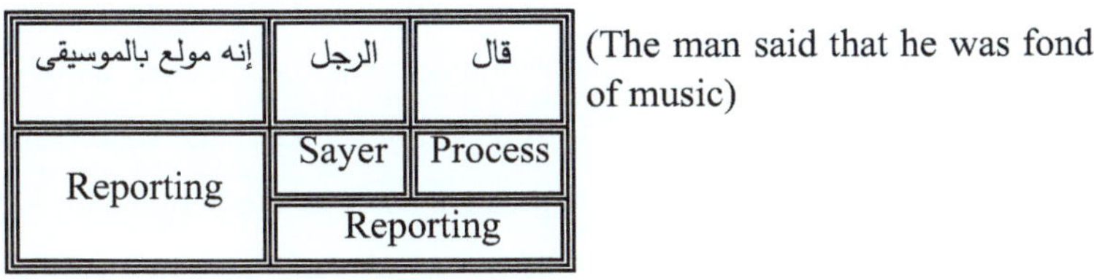

(The man said that he was fond of music)

Figure (37): Examples of verbal processes.

Chapter Three

Contrastive Grammar of English and Arabic

3.1 Subject as a Multifunctional Item in English and Arabic Clauses:

According to Halliday (1994: 30), the subject is a multifunctional item. That is, the subject has different functions depending on three metafunctions: ideational, interpersonal and textual. In other words, the subject could be the concern of the message, and that of which something is predicated, and the doer of the action. Thus, the functions of theme, subject and actor are conflated, i.e. we can have a psychological subject, grammatical subject, and logical subject respectively, e.g.

    a.<u>The boy </u>broke the window.
Theme
Subject

Actor

In (a), 'the boy' is the subject who is the one with whom the message is concerned; the truth or falsehood of the statement is vested in him; and he or she is the one who does the action. So, we can say that the three functions of theme, subject, and actor are conflated in the boy.

In Arabic, the subject is also considered a multifunctional item. In unmarked nominal clause, the inchoative has two functions: the theme & subject, i.e. the psychological and grammatical subject, e.g.

b. حكيم المدير‎   (The manager (is) wise)
Theme
     Subject

It is to be noted that the function of 'actor' in an unmarked nominal clause does not work. Thus, 'المدير' (the manager) can not be regarded as 'actor' in (b). However, in the marked nominal clause the inchoative is no longer a multifunctional item. The role of theme and subject are separated by moving the enunciative in front of the inchoative in the marked nominal clause, the word حكيم (wise) becomes the theme of the clause. Consequently, 'المدير' (the manager) has only one function which is the grammatical subject.

On the other hand, in the unmarked verbal clauses, the agent accomplishes two functions at the same time: subject and actor. Consider the following example:

التفاحة عليّ أكل‎   (lit.) Ate Ali the apple
    Subject   (Ali ate the apple)
   Actor

The two functions of the agent علي (Ali), viz. subject and actor are conflated in علي 'Ali'. Here, Ali is the subject of the clause, i.e. the truth or falsehood of the statement is vested in him. He is also the actor of the action of eating, i.e. the one who does the action of eating.

On the other hand, in the marked verbal clauses, the three functions of the agent are conflated. That is, the agent functions as subject, actor and theme or it is the grammatical, logical and psychological subject:

c. ‏علي أكل تفاحةً.‏
 Theme
 Subject
 Actor

In (c), علي 'Ali' is the <u>Subject</u> of the clause, and it is the <u>Actor</u> who does the action, and it is the <u>Theme</u>, i.e. the one with whom the message is concerned.

3.2 <u>A Comparison of a Clause as a Message in English and Arabic:</u>

1. In both English and Arabic, the theme-rheme organization is positionally determined. In English, the theme occurs at the beginning of the clause, while the rheme is the rest of it. In other words, the theme refers to the starting point of the message, whereas the rheme represents its completion. The same can be said about Arabic clauses in which the theme-rheme organization is

similarly utilized, i.e. the theme occurs at the beginning of the clause. The following examples show this organization in English and Arabic.

a. <u>The man built a new room.</u>
      Th.   Rh.

b. <u>بنىالرجلُ غرفةً جديدةً</u>(lit.) Built the man a new room
     Rh   Th

(The man built a new room)

In (a), the theme is the subject 'the man' which lies at the beginning of the clause. Similarly, in (b) the theme is the verb 'بنى' (built) which also occurs at the beginning of the clause.

2. In addition, in English unmarked pattern, the theme is the subject in declarative clauses, the operator in polar interrogative clauses extending to the following words, the wh-element and the finite verb in imperative clauses. In all these types of clauses, the sequence is Theme-Rheme. In Arabic, however, the clause elements that function as theme in the unmarked pattern are the verbal element in the declarative verbal clauses, the polarity markers (أ) or 'هل' in yes/no questions and the immediately following element, i.e. the verb; the question word in information questions and the following words as well; and the verbal element in directives (Aziz, 1998: 122).

3. It is to be noted that in English, as in Arabic, the process of thematization is realized. That is, the element selected as theme is initially positioned. Strictly speaking, in both English and Arabic, the marked theme is related to the unusual word order. Thus, in

English, by fronting the adverbial group before the subject and the verb, the marked theme is realized, e.g.

a. <u>Yesterday</u> we visited John.

    marked Th.

4. Similarly, in Arabic, the markedness is associated with the unusual sequence of elements of nominal and verbal clauses. That is, in nominal clauses, the usual sequence with the unmarked theme is: inchoative-enunciative, but this order is changed in the marked pattern, e.g.

جائعٌ الطفلُ   (lit.) Hungry (is) the child

                    (The child (is) hungry)

5. English differs from Arabic in that the unmarked theme in Arabic can be changed into marked by agent-verb inversion in verbal clauses which is not the case in English. In other words, Arabic unmarked-marked pattern is determined positionally by the initial element in the structure. For example:

رأت البنت طيراً   (lit.) Saw the girl a bird.

    (The girl saw a bird)

6. Here, the unmarked theme is the verb رأى (saw) in the Arabic structure VSO. By fronting the agent, however, the theme will be marked, i.e. البنت (the girl) is the marked theme:

a. البنت رأت طيراً (The girl saw a bird)

7. It should be noted that this cannot be applied to English. Thus, we cannot say in English:

***b.** Saw the girl a bird.

8. As for the thematic equivalent of the English clause (The girl saw a bird) with (the girl) as unmarked theme, it is not (البنت رأت طيراً). This is due to the fact that the English clause is unmarked, while the Arabic equivalent is marked. Hence, the translator has to seek for the unmarked pattern in Arabic which is equivalent of the English clause (رأت البنت طيراً). This can be illustrated below:

<u>The girl</u> saw a bird.
(English unmarked pattern)

Th.
a. رأت البنت طيراً
(Arabic unmarked pattern)

Th.
b. البنت رأت طيراً
(Arabic marked pattern)

9. On the other hand, English differs from Arabic in that the position of the elements in the Arabic clause is relatively free, so there is a change in the nominal and verbal clauses. For example, in nominal clauses, the thematization of the enunciative is expressed by changing the normal order of the elements of the clause:

كريمٌ الرجلُ   (lit.) Generous (is) the man

(The man (is) generous)

10. Also, in verbal clauses, the thematization of the subject, object or adjunct can be made by changing the usual order of these elements:

a. كتبَ علي الرسالةَ البارحة   (lit.) Wrote Ali the letter yesterday

(Ali wrote the letters yesterday)

b. علي كتب الرسالة البارحة   (Ali wrote the letter yesterday)

(Thematization of the <u>subject</u>)

c.الرسالة كتب(ها) علي البارحة (lit.) The letter wrote Ali yesterday

(The letter was written be Ali yesterday)

(Thematization of the <u>object</u>

d.البارحة كتب علي الرسالة   (lit.) Yesterday wrote Ali the letter

(Yesterday Ali wrote the letter)

(Thematization of the <u>adverb</u>)

11. As shown above, different thematic structures are realized. In (a), the theme is the verb كتب (wrote), while in (b), the thematization of the subject is expressed by fronting the subject in front of the verb. Similarly, in (c), the thematization of the object is utilized by fronting the object to the initial position in the clause. Also, the adjunct in (d) is thematised by a variation in the order of the elements of the clause.

12. So far we have discussed the declarative clauses in English and Arabic. As for the interrogative clauses, however, in both English and Arabic, and especially in polarity questions, there is a two-part theme, i.e. the theme is the operator and extends over the subject:

<u>Didyou</u> call him?
Th(1) Th(2)

هل انت منزعج ؟   (Are you disturbed?)
Th(2) Th(1)

13. With regard to simple and multiple theme in both English and Arabic, the theme may consist of one single nominal group or adverbial group as shown below:

محمدٌ مهندسٌ ناجح   (Mohammed (is) a successful manager)
    simple theme
(NG)

She is here.
simple theme
(NG)

في الدارِ محمد   (Mohammed is at home)
simple theme
  (AG)

Quickly ,he called them.
simple theme
(AG)

3.3 <u>A Comparison of a Clause as Exchange in English and Arabic:</u>

1. In English, the clause is realized as an exchange which corresponds to the interpersonal metafunction. In other words, in communicating with one another, we engage into a number of interpersonal relationships such as making assertions, asking questions, giving orders, etc. Thus, the English clause is realized as an interactive event between the speaker and the hearer.

2. The same is true for Arabic in which the clause is considered as an exchange of giving and demanding. The speaker, here, gives a piece of information to the hearer and he demands something from him.

3.The system of the clause as an exchange in both languages is Mood. However, mood in English is different from that in Arabic. This is due to the structure of both languages. In English, for example, the clause chooses between indicative and imperative moods. The indicative mood makes a choice between interrogative and declarative clause. Thus, (a) and (b) are within the indicative mood.

(a) They went home. (declarative)

(b) Are they happy now? (interrogative)

4. The clauses which are declarative make a choice between tagged and untagged:

 He is a brave man, isn't he? (tagged)

 He is a brave man. (untagged)

5 The interrogative clause makes another choice between closed and open interrogation. Hence,

Have you ever seen him?   is closed interrogation

Where did you go?   is open interrogation

6.As for the imperative clauses, they make choices between exclusive and inclusive imperatives:

a.Close the window! (exclusive)

b. Let's have a walk. (inclusive)

7.In Arabic, however, there are five moods which are the indicative (الرفع), the subjunctive (النصب), the jussive (الجزم), the imperative (الأمر) and the emphatic (التوكيد). The following examples illustrate these moods respectively:

رأيت المدير البارحة

(lit.) Saw I the manager yesterday
(I saw the manager yesterday)
(indicative mood)

لن أساعدك   (lit.) Won't I help you

(I won't help you)
(subjunctive mood)

لم يقرأ محمد الواجب   (lit.) Not read Mohammed the homework
(Mohammed did not read the homework)

(jussive mood)

اقرأ الرسالة   (Read the letter!)
(imperative mood)

لا تذهبنَّ بعيداً   (Don't go too far)
(energetic mood)

8. As for the components of mood, in both English and Arabic, they are two: subject and the finite. As we have mentioned earlier, the subject in Arabic is different from English in that it can be implied in declarative clauses, which is not the case in English.

لا يعرف الجواب   (lit.) Not know the answer
(He doesn't know the answer)

Here, the subject 'هو' 'he' is implied rather than expressed explicitly unless it is stressed:

هو لا يعرف الجواب   (He doesn't know the answer)

9. English declarative clauses cannot be found without a subject. Thus, we cannot say:

Saw Layla Sami.

10.Regarding the second component of the mood, it is expressed by means of tense, modality or polarity features in English and Arabic. Unlike English, Arabic has no distinction between auxiliaries and lexical verbs. Also, there are no modal verbs which realize modality. Instead, there are different words and expressions which are used to express modality and modulation. The meanings of modality are certainty, possibility which are expressed by ينبغي، يجب and لابد أن; while the major meanings of modulation are expressed by ability, permission and obligation which are conveyed by verbs such as يستطيع، يتمكن, etc. The difference between English and Arabic with this respect can be shown below:

She <u>can</u> speak English fluently. (ability)

(ability)   <u>تستطيع ان</u> تتكلم الإنكليزية بطلاقة

11. We can, then, say that the finite component of the Arabic clause includes expressions and particles which express modality and modulation such as لن، لم، لابد أن، يجب.

12.So far we have dealt with the components of the mood which are the subject and the finite. The rest of the English clause which is similar to Arabic is termed the residue. The analysis of these two clauses are diagrammed below:

The secretary	has	typed the letter for 3 hours
Subject	Finite	
Mood		Residue

Figure (38): A structure of English declarative clause as an exchange.

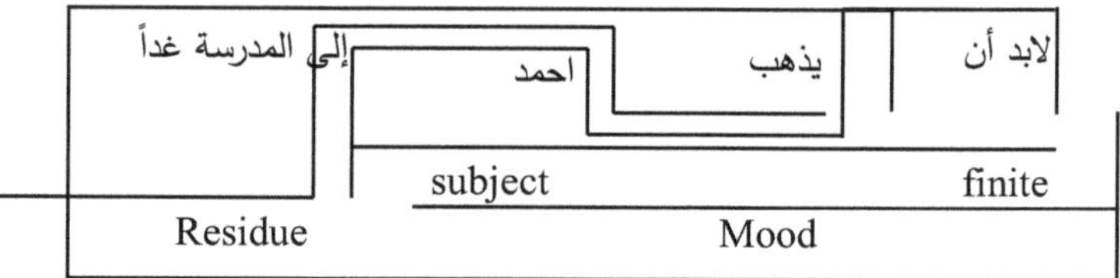

Figure (39): A structure of Arabic declarative clause as an exchange.

12. Moreover, unlike English in which the operators are utilized to negate and interrogate declarative clauses, Arabic uses particles such as لا، لن، لم to make negative clauses. Consequently, these particles are considered within the finite element of the Arabic verbal clause, e.g.

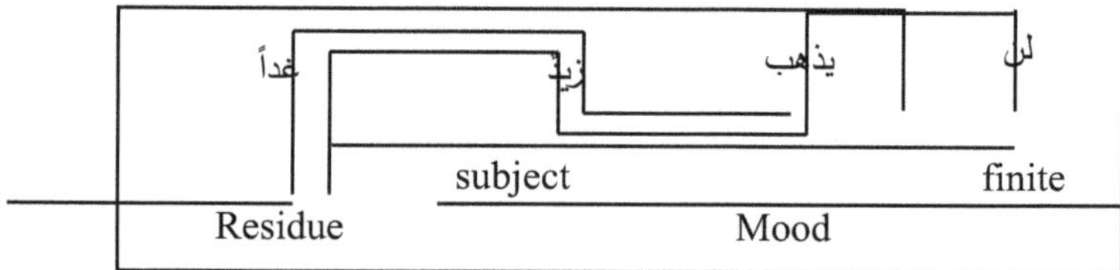

Figure (40): A structure of unmarked Arabic declarative clause.

13. It should be noted, here, that this structure is clearly expressed by the marked pattern as shown below:

a.

يذهب غداً	لن	زيدٌ
Residue	finite	subject

Figure (41): A structure of marked Arabic clause.

3.4<u>A Comparison of English and Arabic Clauses as Representation:</u>

1. In English, the clause is realized in its experiential or ideational metafunction, i.e. its use as a means by which we represent patterns of experience. Following Halliday (1994: 107), the process consists of three components: the process, the participants and the circumstances in which the process takes place. For example:

a. The boy broke the window yesterday.

'the boy', in (a), is the participant, the verb 'broke' is the process and 'yesterday' is the circumstance. This can be shown below:

The boy	Broke	the window	Yesterday
Participant	Process	Goal	Circumstance

Figure (42): A structure of English clause as a representation.

2.The same can be said about only Arabic verbal clauses which are modes of reflection the events. The grammatical system of transitivity, following Halliday (ibid.), construes the experience of the world into process types. Similar to English clauses, the process is made up of three components: the process, the participant and the circumstance:

(lit.) Received the student the present happily استلم الطالبُ الهديةَ فرحاً

(The student received the present happily)

Here, the verb, 'استلم' 'received' is the process, 'الطالبُ' 'the student' is the participant and 'فَرِحاً' 'happily' is the circumstance related to the process. This can be illustrated in figure (43).

فَرِحاً	الهدية	الطالبُ	استلمَ
Circumstance	Goal	Participant	Process

Figure (43): A structure of Arabic clause as a representation.

3.Turning back to subject (or what is called participant), it is differently termed in accordance with the process in which it occurs. In material processes, in both English and Arabic, the subject is called the <u>Actor</u> with or with no goal. In other words, in clauses with intransitive verbs, there is only an actor with no goal. The English and Arabic examples are given below:

<u>The childslept</u>

  Actor   Process

نامالطفلُ   (lit.) Slept the child

Actor   Process   (The child slept.)

4.As for clauses of transitive verbs, there is a second participant that is termed 'goal'. Consider:

<u>The girlkickedthe ball.</u>

  Actor Process Goal

درسَ الولدُ الدرسَ   (lit.) Studied the boy the lesson

(The boy studied the lesson.)

One further point is that in both English and Arabic, these processes are called 'processes of doing'. That is, in English, we can test the Actor by questioning 'what did x do?' or 'what did x do to'. The same can be said about Arabic by making the following questions ' ماذا فعل فلان؟' or ' ماذا فعل فلان لـ فلان؟'.

5.In the mental processes (or processes of sensing), the subject in the English clause is called <u>'Sensor'</u> who is the one who sense, feels and thinks. Thus, the sensor should be a human being who is conscious, e.g.

<u>He   hates</u>me.
Sensor   Process   Phenomenon

6.The rest of the clause apart from the Sensor and the Process is the Phenomenon.

7.Similarly, in Arabic mental process, the sensor must be human who senses and feels, e.g.

عرفَ عليُ الجواب   (lit.) Knew Ali the answer

(Ali knew the answer)

8.Moreover, different subtypes of mental processes are realized in English and Arabic which are: verbs of perception like see (رأى), hear (سمع), verbs of affection like love (أحب); and verbs of cognition such as know (عرف) and understand (فهم).

9.On the other hand, in the behavioural processes, the subject in English and Arabic is called <u>'Behaver'</u>. These processes are partly like

93

the material and partly like the mental. The 'behaver' is human but the process is something like that of 'doing', e.g.

<u>The man</u> laughed.
behaver

رقصت <u>البنت</u> فرحاً   (lit.) Danced the girl merrily

behaver   (The girl danced merrily.)

10.Finally, in verbal processes which are called 'processes of saying', the subject is the one who is saying something. Thus, it is labelled 'Sayer':

<u>Helen said,</u>   ' I'm glad.'
Sayer   Process   Quoted

11. In indirect (or reported speech), the reported words are expressed by a subordinate clause attached to the reporting one. In indirect (or reported speech), the reported words are expressed by a subordinate clause attached to the reporting one. Thus, the above clause will be :

<u>Helen said</u>   that <u>she was glad</u>
Sayer process   reported

In Arabic clauses, the subject is the Sayer in both quoting and reporting clauses. Similarly, the reporting clause is expressed by a subordinate clause, e.g.

قال <u>محمد</u>: "<u>إنني متعب</u>"   (lit.) Said Mohammed: 'I am tired'
   Quoted   Sayer   Process   (Mohammed said: "I am tired")
قال <u>محمد</u> إنه متعب   (lit.) Said Mohammed he is tired
Reported   Sayer   Process   (Mohammed said that he is tired.")

12.English is similar to Arabic in that the theme combines three types of meanings which realize three metafunctions: ideational, interpersonal and textual. That is, the English and Arabic clauses are merely representations of experience, interactive exchanges and messages. Consequently, in both languages, the components of the multiple theme are: textual theme, interpersonal theme, and ideational (or topical) theme. This point can be shown in the examples below:

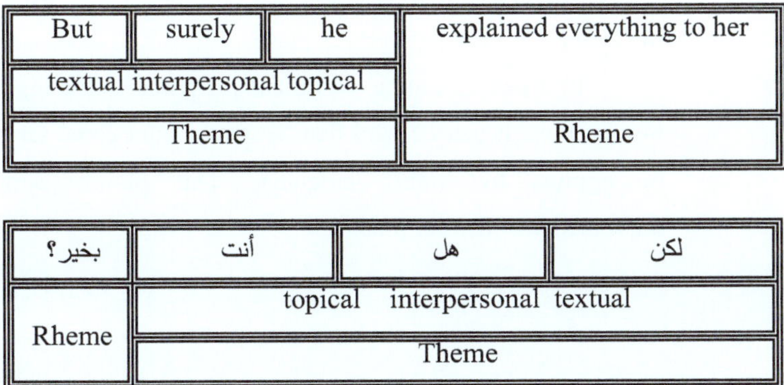

But	surely	he	explained everything to her
textual	interpersonal	topical	
Theme			Rheme

بخير؟	أنت	هل	لكن
Rheme	topical	interpersonal	textual
	Theme		

Figure (44): Examples of multiple theme in English and Arabic

Unlike English, the ideational (or topical) theme which is the implied subject may not be found in multiple theme in Arabic. Thus, the structure of Arabic multiple theme may combine only textual and interpersonal themes. Consider:

سافر في العطلة؟	أين	حسنٌ
Rheme	interpersonal	textual
	Theme	

Figure (45): An example of multiple theme with interpersonal and textual themes

However, simple and multiple themes have been found in English and Arabic clauses. The theme may consist of one single nominal or adverbial group. Also, the theme may combine three metafunctions: textual, interpersonal and ideational or topical. In English, the three components of the multiple theme have to be found in the clause, while in Arabic, the multiple theme may have two components: textual and interpersonal. This is the case when the agent is implied in verbal clauses.

In a sense, similar and different points were highlighted in this chapter. It can be said that Systemic Functional Grammar can be applied to Arabic language. This plainly supports the universality of the approach.

References

Abdulla, M. A. (1991). **Thematic   Organization in English and Arabic**. Unpublished M.A. Thesis. Mosul: University of Mosul

Al-Makhzumi, M. (1966). **Fi nnhawil'Arabi:a'idwaTatbiq 'ala l-Manhajil-'Ilmiyyil-Hadith**. Cairo: Mattba'atu Mustafa l-Halabi.

Aziz, Y. Y. (1989). **A Contrastive Grammar of English and Arabic**. Mosul: University of Mosul

-------------- (1997). **Al-Ma'nawa l-Tarjama**. Banghzi: ManshuratJami'atuQarYunis.

___________ (1998). **Topics in Translation with Special Reference to English and Arabic**. Benghazi: ManshuratJami'atQarYounis

Berry, M. (1975). **An Introduction to Systemic Linguistics: Structures and Systems**, Vol.2. London: B.T. Batsford Ltd

Booth, W. C. (1961). **The Rhetoric of Fiction**. Chicago: University of Chicago Press

Butler, C. S. (1985). **Systemic Linguistics Theory and Applications**. London: Bastford Academic and Educational.

Crystal,D.(1985).**A Dictionary of Linguistics and Phonetics**. Oxford: Blackwell.

Dowing A. and Lock, P. (2002). **A University Course in English Grammar**. London & New York: Routledge
Farhan, Z. G. (1999). **Syntactic Structures in Relation to Thematic Progression in Arabic with Special Reference to English**. Unpublished Ph.D. Thesis. Mosul: University of Mosul.

Fawcett, R. P., Tucker G. H. and Lin, Y. C. (1993). **How a Systemic Functional Grammar Works.**

Galbraith, J. K. (1988). "The Military: A Loose Cannon?" In: S. Day and E. Mcmahan (eds.), **The Writer's Resources**: 307-310. New York: McGraw Hill

Kress, G. R. (1976). **Halliday: System and Function in Language**. London: Oxford University Press.

Halliday, M. A. K. (1967). "Notes on Transitivity and Theme in English" Parts 1, 2 and 3. **Journal of Linguistics** 3.1, 3.2, 4.2: 199-244.

___________________ (1970). Language Structure and Language Function. In: J. Lyons (ed.), **New Horizons in Linguistics**, London: Harmondsworth, Middx: Penguin Books.

___________________ (1985). **An Introduction to Functional Grammar**. (1st edition). London: Edward Arnold.

_________________ (1994). **An Introduction to Functional Grammar**. (2nd edition). London: Edward Arnold_________ (1985). **A Dictionary of Linguistics and Phonetics**. Oxford: Blackwell.

Halliday, M. K. And Matthiessen ,C.M.(2004).**An Introduction to Functional Grammar.** (3rd edition).London:Hodder Education

Hudson, R. A. (1970). **English Complex Sentences: An Introduction to Systemic Grammar**. London: North-Holland Publishing Company

Hutchins, W. J. (1975). Subjects, Themes and Case Grammars. **Lingua** 35, 101-133, North-Holland Publishing Company.

Kopple, W. J. (1991). "Themes, Thematic Progressions, and Some Implications for Understanding Discourse". **Written Communication**, Vol.8, No.3: 311-347. London: SAGE Publications, Inc

Kress, G. R. (1976). **Halliday: System and Function in Language**. London: Oxford University Press

Mahfuz, N. (1974). **Miramar** (2nd edition). Beirut: Dar ul-Qalam.

Mattissen and Halliday, M. A. K. (1997). "Systemic Functional Grammar: A First Step into the Theory".

Quirk, R.; Greenbaum, S.; Leech, G. and Svartvik, J. (1985). **A Comprehensive Grammar of English**. London: Longman.

Muir, J. (1972). **A Modern Approach to English Grammar**. London: Bastford.

Wright, W. (1971). **A Grammar of Arabic Language**. Cambridge: Cambridge University Press.

Printed by Books on Demand GmbH, Norderstedt / Germany